PROFESSIONAL
MODELLING

PROFESSIONAL MODELLING

Louise Cole and Giles Vickers-Jones

First published in 2009 by New Holland Publishers (UK) Ltd
London • Cape Town • Sydney • Auckland

Garfield House
86-88 Edgware Road
London W2 2EA
United Kingdom
www.newhollandpublishers.com

80 McKenzie Street
Cape Town 8001
South Africa

Unit 1
66 Gibbes Street
Chatswood
NSW 2067
Australia

218 Lake Road
Northcote
Auckland
New Zealand

ISBN 978 1 84773 056 5

Senior Editor **Corinne Masciocchi**
Designer **Isobel Gillan**
Studio photographer **Andy Lesauvage**
Production **Marion Storz**
Editorial Direction **Rosemary Wilkinson**

10 9 8 7 6 5 4 3 2 1

Reproduction by Pica Digital PTE Ltd, Singapore
Printed and bound by Craft Print International Ltd, Singapore

contents

introduction

Today, modelling is seen not only as a glamorous and exciting profession, but also as a legitimate career. The world of modelling can offer fantastic opportunities to travel the world, meet lots of interesting people and potentially earn fantastic amounts of money.

Most people are familiar with fashion and catwalk modelling but what you may not realise is that there are many different types of modelling, including glamour, teen, body, sports, plus size, petite, real people, pregnancy, family and baby, and even unusual/freaks! So if for whatever reason, you feel you do not fit into the more obvious categories (because you do not meet the required height and weight criteria for instance), there are always other options available. Here, we aim to show you how you can find your very own place, whether it's high fashion or feet, and work professionally within this amazingly diverse industry.

We have both been involved in many aspects of modelling, including catwalk, advertising, magazine work, catalogues and commercials, however, when we first started out there was no handbook to guide us. We had to find our own way and we both made mistakes; some of them were costly, some just wasted precious time and more than a few were fairly embarrassing! This book will help you avoid the pitfalls and contains all the information you need to help you get the best out of this industry with straightforward, honest advice.

In Chapter 2 we cover the different types of modelling, with a look at each category, from plus size to high fashion. Chapter 3 explains how to find a good agent. We look at the different ways to approach an agency and how to decide which one suits you best. Chapter 4 offers invaluble advice on how to build your portfolio, find a trustworthy photographer, win your castings and what to expect on your first job. Chapter 5 teaches you how to pose according to the type of modellling you are doing, whether it is fashion, catalogue or bridal and also how to master the runway walk! Chapter 6 looks at working abroad. Modelling markets differ from country to country so we explain where is best to work and when. Chapter 7 is all about grooming and exercise as healthy living is vital to being a successful model. As a model you are self employed, so Chapter 8 covers finances as it is important to know how and when to pay tax as well as managing your own accounts. Chapter 9 offers valuable advice on longetivity as a model and future prospects, as well as alternative careers. Finally, there is also a glossary explaining less known modelling terms and a useful contacts page listing worldwide reputable agencies.

Modelling isn't just about the way you look, it's also about having a great personality and a great attitude. Useful hints and tips on all this and more will help you make the most of your chosen career. The modelling industry today is highly competitive and it is likely that you will have to learn to deal with rejection before you find success. We will help you through these difficult early stages, show you the right people to go to and how to approach them. Good luck!

LOUISE AND GILES

modelling through the ages

A model is defined as a person who poses for art, fashion, products or advertising, and who helps create an image for a product to establish desirability and demand in order to sell that product to consumers.

Over the years the requirements of models and the preferred 'look' (what is considered beautiful and fashionable) have changed considerably. The fashion industry, which embraces designers and manufacturers, magazine editors, advertisers, photographers, hairstylists, make-up artists and stylists, is constantly redefining the look to keep consumers interested and keen to buy.

Modelling today offers opportunities to many different types of models. Clients want new faces and fresh looks, and instead of one type of model covering all aspects of modelling, different models are now booked for their specialised area, for instance, hands or swimwear.

When clients pick models, they base their choices on a range of influences from the world of art, politics and culture, and as these areas are in constant flux, so are the requirements for models. The Internet has had a major impact on the advertising world and has altered the way a model's career has traditionally developed. Models no longer have to travel the world to get noticed, and can be based in one place whilst still being successful worldwide.

Trends in photography also affect the modelling industry, with gritty close-up shots of more 'real' looking models being preferred today. One headshot of a certain type of person, for instance a student, is expected to represent a whole group of people for an advertisement.

So why do fashions change? In modern westernised societies, ideals of beauty and fashion change over time, with different parts of the body being emphasised at different times. Barely two centuries ago, plumpness was considered attractive and a sign of wealth and beauty. Artists' paintings suggest that from the 15th to the 18th centuries fat was erotic and fashionable. The uncertainty of food supplies and regular famines meant a plump body indicated that the father or husband was prosperous.

In Victorian times, models drawn for magazines had a tiny waist, and girls were squeezed into corsets to accentuate the hips. After 1900 the large bottom was in fashion and women wore bustles. Later in the 1920s, after WWI, women had enough of simply being child bearers and wanted to have fun. Fashions changed, dresses became shorter and being thin was fashionable.

At the same time in the United States photography was professionalised, a development that paralleled the growth of modern advertising. Fashion houses wanted photographers to take pictures of their latest designs worn by beautiful people, and so the first fashion models came into being.

Between the 1920s and 1950s it was not necessarily models that women wanted to emulate but film stars, such as Marilyn Monroe who was curvy and far from what is currently regarded as ideal. The 1960s were all about youth and flower power. Young people were rebelling against the establishment, and fashion changed dramatically with mini skirts, go-go boots and lots of heavy eye make-up being all

A lady in Victorian attire, where small waistlines were in fashion. Marilyn Monroe's curvaceous figure was all the rage in the 1950s.

the rage. It was at this time that the slim, boy-like body became fashionable, and Twiggy (who weighed only 44 kg /97 lbs) took the fashion scene by storm with her tiny frame, pixie haircut and big eyes. During this decade, Donyale Luna was the first African American model to appear in Vogue magazine.

In the 1970s disco music, platform shoes and bellbottoms became popular. The TV show Charlie's Angels popularised independence and healthy bodies for women, and Farrah Fawcett became the face of this decade. Models Beverly Johnson, Janice Dickinson, Cheryl Tiegs, Jerry Hall, Christie Brinkley and Lauren Hutton also became recognisable to the general public.

The 1980s were about money – gold, glitz and glamour. Fashion houses such as Chanel and Yves Saint Laurent established themselves during this decade and everyone wanted designer labels. The economy was booming and branding was everywhere (as were shoulder pads and big hairstyles!). Exercise became popular as did bright Lycra sportswear. Fashion designers began advertising on television and billboards, and models such as Christie Brinkley became familiar to the public, replacing movie stars as the symbols of luxury and wealth.

The 1990s was the decade of minimalism, and baggy trousers, leggings, Chinese cheongsam dresses and grunge fashions were everywhere. It was during this decade that supermodels became increasingly prominent in the media. These highly-paid elite fashion models had a worldwide reputation and often a background in haute couture and commercial modelling. Supermodels worked for top fashion designers and labels and secured multi-million dollar contracts and campaigns. They became household names with worldwide recognition.

Lisa Fonssagrives is considered the world's first supermodel. She featured in most of the major fashion magazines from the 1930s to the 1950s and appeared on over 200 covers of Vogue. Although many models were referred to as supermodels during the 1990s, only six were officially recognised and accepted by the fashion world: Claudia Schiffer, Cindy Crawford, Kate Moss, Linda Evangelista, Naomi Campbell and Christy Turlington. They were the most sought after, collectively dominating magazine covers, fashion runways, editorial pages, and both print and broadcast advertising.

A young Kate Moss cuts an iconic figure on the catwalk.

Tyson Beckford, one of the world's most popular male supermodels.

These supermodels were to be seen on talk shows, in movie roles, partying at the trendiest nightclubs, dating rock stars and earning millions of dollars. Their fame empowered them to take charge of their careers and command higher fees.

When Linda Evangelista said in a Vogue interview in 1990 that 'we don't get out of bed for less than $10,000 a day', this comment became the most notorious in modelling history. In 1991, Christy Turlington signed a contract with Maybelline that paid her $800,000 for twelve days' work each year.

Men's fashion represents just a fraction of the industry and male supermodels such as Marcus Schenkenberg, Tyson Beckford, Will Chalker and Mark Vanderloo have not been able to command similar salaries.

By the year 2000, actors, athletes, musicians, reality TV stars, pop singers and other celebrities began replacing supermodels on fashion magazine covers and in advertising campaigns. Even designers turned to models who were less glamorous and lesser known so they would not eclipse their designs. The era of the supermodel was coming to an end. In this decade Gisele Bündchen has been the only model close to earning the title of supermodel.

01 types of modelling

types of modelling

Before you approach an agency it is important to determine which type of modelling is right for you. There are many different types of modelling so if you are not naturally slim, do not starve yourself to fit the fashion model ideal. Instead, believe in what you have to offer rather than trying to drastically change yourself, and concentrate on finding an area that suits you.

Catwalk and fashion

These are the tall, skinny models you see on the catwalks and on the fashion pages of magazines. Catwalk models model clothes in fashion shows whereas fashion modelling covers a wide range of work, from editorials and covers for fashion magazines to commercial advertising campaigns for manufacturers. They usually have an edgy current look and must meet the height and size criteria which are determined each year by the designers' sample clothing. In recent years, the ideal female fashion model is between 16 and 21 years old, 1.80 m (5 ft 11 in) tall and weighs 54 kg (8.5 stone). These requirements have changed considerably since the 1980s, when slighter bigger sizes were in fashion.

In general, however, female catwalk models are aged between 16 and 21 and range between 1.75 m (5 ft 9 in) and 1.80 m (5 ft 11 in). The waist should be around 60 cm (24 in) and the hip size 86 cm (34 in). The clothes size should range between a US 0 and 6 (UK 4 and 10). Breast size is also important, with cup sizes no bigger than a B in order to fit the sample clothing. Female catwalk models tend to be young, mainly because they must look as good in real life as they would under studio lights after retouching. At this age the skin is flawless and there are few or no unsightly lumps and bumps.

Male catwalk models are aged between 16 and 25, and are between 1.82 m (6 ft) and 1.88 m (6 ft 2 in) tall. The ideal waist measurement is 81 cm (32 in) with a 100–106 cm (40–42 in) chest. There has been a recent trend for designers to demonstrate their clothes on skinny looking men but in general men tend to be nicely toned but not too muscular, to ensure the sample clothing fits to perfection.

Whilst the ideal size and weight requirements may vary from year to year, height specifications for fashion models are fairly rigid as most designers feel their clothes hang best on taller models. Another reason for keeping to a strict height requirement is to ensure consistency on photo shoots – a much shorter model would look out of place in amongst his or her taller peers.

Today, more and more clients want unique fresh faces. The preferred look in fashion models may be vastly different from one year to the next, and as a result last season's top models may not work the next.

With the advent of the Internet, clients have access to a much wider selection of models from all over the world from which to make their choice. The Internet and worldwide media have also led to more cross-cultural influences so it is very hard to determine which look will be fashionable from year to year. For instance, a Japanese blockbuster film could influence next season's look and the models required would need to be dark haired with an oriental flavour.

Commercial

'Commercial' refers to the type of assignment: the objective is to sell a product or service and this will be reflected in the final image. Commercial models tend to have a more attainable look than high fashion models. They can advertise all sorts of products, ranging from cars, mobile phones, cleaning and beauty products to banking and insurance – pretty much anything and everything! They often represent the average consumer, only more attractive.

Height and size requirements are not as rigid as for fashion models but they must still be very well proportioned. Men and women as short as 1.70 m (5 ft 7 in) have been known to do well in this division.

The commercial market is very lucrative for models, and although it is seen as less glamorous than fashion modelling it can often offer a much longer and more successful career.

Commercial models often have that 'boy-/girl-next-door' look and can work at almost any age, from young teenagers to those well into their 80s! Ethnic models tend to do very well in this market as clients wish to reflect our modern multi-cultural society and appeal to the widest possible market.

For most advertising jobs, the commercial model is expected to take to the shoot a wide selection of clothes. This is so the client can choose the clothes to complement their product, knowing they fit the model well, and this also helps to reduce their costs. The clothes must be plain with no logos or graphics, and clients usually prefer neutral shades and nothing too trendy, as these tend to date too quickly. You can't, however, be expected to own everything so if a specific and unusual item is required, for instance a yellow spotted shirt, the client will supply this.

TV commercials

There is no one specific look for TV commercials. Age, size, build, ethnicity, accent and gender will all depend on the products being advertised.

Models tend to be used for non-speaking commercials. For instance, a fashion model will be used for beauty products and hair advertisements. More commercial models advertise holiday destinations, cars and other luxury goods. For speaking parts in commercials actors are the preferred choice. However, if you fit the brief you will often get an audition.

for girls

THE BASIC WARDROBE CONSISTS OF:

- Plain shoes with a medium heel, in black and white
- Selection of tights, including flesh-coloured and black
- Underwear (knickers and bras), flesh-coloured as well as white and black
- Trousers, in black and beige
- Plain skirts, in black and beige
- Selection of blouses/shirts, casual and smart, short and long sleeved, in white and in blue
- Dresses, an evening and a day dress
- Selection of suits, one smart trouser or skirt suit in black
- T-shirts
- Jeans
- Sportswear, such as a track suit, gym wear, swimsuit, bikini and clean white trainers
- Coats, casual and smart, in neutral shades
- Nightwear, in neutral colours
- Accessories, to include belts, jewellery, hats, gloves, handbags and hairclips

for boys

THE BASIC WARDROBE CONSISTS OF:

- Shoes, in black and brown
- Tight fitting underwear
- Trousers, casual and smart, in black and beige
- Selection of shirts, casual and smart, short and long sleeved, particularly in white and blue
- Selection of suits (light and dark colours)
- Plain ties
- T-shirts
- Jeans
- Sportswear, such as a track suit, gym wear, swimming shorts and white trainers
- Sweatshirts and polo shirts
- Coats, casual and smart, in neutral shades
- Nightwear, vest and shorts, in neutral colours

Commercials also use walk-on and background artistes, supplied by specialist agencies and model agencies.

Commercials can be very lucrative for models and one commercial alone can be enough to support a model for a year. Commercials are often paid by 'usage', which means that the model receives money each time the ad is televised, so if the ad is popular the model will do extremely well from it.

Children and family

Children's modelling is generally grouped into baby, toddler and children up to age 12 (in looks rather than actual age). The work is varied and includes toy magazines, parenting magazines, games, catalogues, medication products, children's charities, TV commercials and fashion shows.

Child models must be happy and smiley, with clear skin and bright eyes. Not all have to be pretty or cute; sometimes a quirky look with plenty of character is preferred. It is, however, important that all baby and child models are good natured, co-operative and sociable, as modelling will mean meeting and working with lots of strangers. Temper tantrums and bad manners will not be tolerated. It is also important that children and parents alike have the ability to cope with rejection and not to take it personally.

Working as a young model can help a child gain confidence. However, parents must keep their child's best interests in mind and not live their dreams through their child. Encourage your child if this is what he/she wants to do and always keep the atmosphere fun and light-hearted or the child will not enjoy the experience and will not perform

well for the camera. Also do consider the effect it will have on your other children: modelling assignments may require you to spend a lot of time out on jobs and castings with your child, as children must be accompanied at all times when they are working and this can create an element of jealousy and sibling rivalry.

As children change and grow so quickly (teeth falling out, new hairstyles, braces, etc.) their pictures rapidly date so almost all jobs require a casting, to which children will need chaperoning. Expenses are generally covered by the client and a small fee is usually paid to the child for attending the casting.

Castings are often held after school but jobs tend to be on a school day so it is important to be selective over which jobs to take as children are only allowed a certain number of days off school per year to work. In most countries the laws on child licensing state that any person under school-leaving age must be licensed to work in modelling and entertainment. This is a matter for the agency to address along with the child's guardian.

Baby and child modelling can be a lot of fun and a great record to look back on as your child grows. You must, however, be prepared for a lot of waiting around at castings and on jobs and realise that clients will not tolerate pushy parents. For this reason, children are often cast as much for the parent as for the look of the child. There is nothing worse than an overbearing parent on a job all day!

Many child models are the children of adult models. Generally, this is because the parents already know about the industry and how to behave and have a flexible working schedule that allows them to attend castings. It can be difficult for a working parent to attend castings and arrange babysitters if required. That said, it is acceptable to take your other children to castings and jobs and there is usually a play area to accommodate them.

The modelling agencies that represent children also often have a family section where clients can book an entire family for adverts, such as holidays, theme parks and household products. Occasionally real life families are used, but more often than not the children are grouped with a model mum and dad.

Teens

Over the past decade teenage models have become more and more popular as the number of magazines and products targeted at teens has grown. Teen models are both male and female and are a more attractive version of the everyday teenager. They must look between 15 and 17 years old and some models in their early 20s manage to remain in this market as they photograph a lot younger than their years.

Teen models are slim and in proportion and can be shorter than fashion models. Their look tends to be more wholesome than that of edgy high fashion models. Here the emphasis is on clear skin, bright eyes and a warm smile. In some cases a more normal looking teenager is required and sometimes even dental braces are acceptable. Teenagers are usually photographed with minimal make-up and simply styled hair, and work mainly for teen magazines and catalogues.

Glamour

Glamour modelling is the dream of many young girls as it can be a way of achieving celebrity status. It differs from fashion and commercial modelling in that it represents a lifestyle and image rather than advertising clothes or a product.

These models must be in proportion although tend to be under the 1.75 m (5 ft 9 in) minimum fashion model height requirement and have larger breasts than the preferred B cup. They do topless or more explicit sexy pictures, for example swimsuit and nude modelling. Work includes newspapers, lads' magazines and underwear catalogues. Other types of work include personal appearances at events such as motor racing, showbiz parties and music videos.

Glamour models in particular must be very careful when it comes to syndication rights to their pictures and should be well versed in the legalities involved. This is when a model signs away the picture rights to one or more photographer or client who can then legally sell them on to publication picture buyers. This can often lead to a model being overpowered or not recovering the money they should for the level of exposure achieved. The model loses all control of where and for what purpose the pictures are published. So make sure you are fully aware of the facts before signing any contractual agreement.

Pregnancy modelling

Although there are a few agencies that specialise in pregnant women, most clients will in fact go to one of the larger commercial or fashion modelling agencies. As there are numerous models on their books, there will usually be a few models who are pregnant.

Specialist pregnancy agencies often look for women from various backgrounds, whether they have previous modelling experience or are just photogenic, ensuring the need for prosthetic bumps is a thing of the past!

There are many mother and baby magazines, clothing companies and baby products manufacturers that require models of all ages and sizes, from about the fourth month of pregnancy onwards.

It is important when considering pregnancy modelling that you can be flexible with your time and that you have adequate transport. You will be requested to go on castings for jobs, which may be tricky on packed commuter trains! Towards the end of your pregnancy clients will often send cars to collect you and take you home after jobs.

Plus sizes and petites

Plus size models are usually female, with a minimum dress size 12, and around 1.75 m (5 ft 9 in) tall. Although larger than fashion and commercial models (they are usually a US size 12, UK size 16), they must still have a well-proportioned body. Work includes specialist catalogues and fashion shows. Plus size models are also used on many TV show fashion segments to more realistically represent the average consumer.

Petite models are usually female and 1.65 m (5 ft 5 in) and under in height and a US dress size 2–6 (UK size 6–8). Work is limited but there are opportunities for fittings and catalogues for the petite designer range.

Fittings models

These models have what is considered well proportioned body measurements for clothes to be fitted to by designers before the final articles go into the shops. Women are usually a perfect US size 6 (UK 10) and 1.75 m (5 ft 9 in) in height with a good waist to hip ratio. Men are usually 1.82 m (6 ft) tall with an 81 cm (32 in) chest, but these averages do vary according to the market.

Fittings models do not need to be as photogenic as fashion and commercial models. It is essential, however, that their weight and size do not fluctuate as they should be able to say when a garment is either too tight or too loose for the size they are being fitted for.

All designers need their clothes fitted so there is a lot of work around for these types of models and there are no age restrictions. Although day rates are not as high as for fashion modelling, if you are good you can work almost every day, going from designer to designer, as bookings are usually made for two to three months at a time.

In-house modelling

These models show the new season's clothes of high end and high street fashion houses to fashion buyers. Buyers come to a fashion house and pick the outfits of interest and the models then model the outfits.

These models must fit the sample size. This varies from country to country but for women it is usually a US size 4 or 6 (UK size 8 or 10) and 1.75 m (5 ft 9 in) in height. Men should have an 81 cm (32 in) chest, a 76 cm (30 in) waist and be 1.83 m (6 ft) tall.

Often the clients have allocated one-hour time slots to view the clothes but sometimes clients are free to turn up at a time that is convenient to them, which means that as a model you are on call all day.

In-house modelling can be quite tedious as you will have to constantly change in and out of clothes and spend most of your day in a changing room. On the other hand, it can be extremely lucrative as you often get booked for week-long slots, and fashion houses tend to find a model they like and re-book again and again. Also if there is a gap between client meetings you will often be allowed to go on your castings and start late or finish early.

Parts and body models

For this type of modelling any part of the body can be used, from hands and feet to ears, eyes and hair. These models are often used in films, where an actor's body parts are played by a double. You do not need any specific training for this type of work, however, you are expected to be professional on set, good at taking direction and quick to re-position.

Although there are many agencies that specialise in body parts, the majority of models doing this sort of work are those signed to a modelling agency but who also happen to have great hands or perfect feet.

Some parts models, however, are extremely skilled in motion technique. For instance, reaching out and picking up a product over and over again, hitting the same mark in exactly the same way can be can take a lot of practice.

Body modelling is primarily for male models who are more bulked up than the average men's fashion or commercial model. They still need to be 1.80 m (5 ft 11 in) to 1.88 m (6 ft 2 in) tall and in proportion. Female body models tend to work through a general modelling agency. However, men may find more work via a more specific body model agency.

Jobs vary from magazine editorials to cologne advertisements, sportswear catalogues and even calendars. Because their faces are often included in the shot, it is rare for a body model to get away with a good physique alone.

Often clients and creative directors will have a very definite pose they want copied and it is often a difficult one to hold and recreate so they need the skills of a body model. Body models must also be able to accentuate different parts of the body and know how their body will look best on camera. For instance, exhaling when posing tightens abdominal muscles and makes a real difference in pictures.

Look-alikes

Do you get told you look like a celebrity? Look-a-likes agencies represent models who look like actors, politicians, singers, royalty, models and TV stars.

Work includes TV and film work, media events, conferences, adverts, corporate functions, store and shopping centre openings, charity appearances, award ceremonies, product launches, fêtes, weddings, private parties and magazine shoots. Rates of pay vary depending on the popularity of the celebrity you look like.

There is also work available for people who can imitate a celebrity's voice. This varies from radio adverts and mobile ring tones to joke phone calls. Some talented celebrity look-alikes get together and form a tribute band, often touring with gigs around the world.

Promotional work

These models attend events on behalf of clients and are very friendly, outgoing and sociable. They tend not to be as photogenic as models but are still very pretty. Work includes handing out flyers for events, working on promotional stands at exhibitions, field marketing, hospitality, sampling and merchandising, hosting motorsport events, and hosting tables at dinners. Many models, actors and dancers do promotional work to supplement their income. It can be a great way to meet lots of interesting people and a chance to attend some fun events, such as music concerts, sporting events, seasonal festivals, and boat shows.

Promotional models can be male or female between the ages of 18 and 40 and must be outgoing, friendly and enthusiastic. Uniforms are usually supplied by the client, and come in various styles, from branded T-shirts to character outfits, but you will be told by your agent what exactly is required before agreeing to the job. Promotional work is often booked for a few days or even weeks at a time.

Classic modelling

These are older models, aged 40 or over, and they tend to model for luxury and often high-paying clients, such as car and holiday companies. As consumers get older their buying power often increases, and advertisers like to target them with similarly aged models. Therefore, classic models can look their age and have a few wrinkles – however not the type caused by ill health or excessive smoking!

Many models in this division were models in their younger days and gave up modelling either to pursue other careers or to have a family, and decide to go back to it at a later stage. Some even find they work more as an older model. Work includes fashion shows, catalogues and advertising products.

Couples

Some clients prefer to use real life couples in their advertisements because they feel the models look more comfortable together and therefore more believable in the pictures. The work is very varied and includes magazine advertising, Valentines shoots and romantic holidays, to name a few. Commercial-looking models work best for this type of work and couples can be of any age.

With holiday brochure companies couples are often flown abroad for shoots. Not only are the real life couples often easier to direct, but clients can also save money by not having to book two separate rooms! Some models have been known to pretend to be real life couples for this sort of work!

Real people

Real people models or 'character' models represent real-looking consumers, such as a van driver for a breakdown advert, a florist selling flowers, a fireman driving a fire engine, a businessman at the photocopier, a nerdy train spotter and even Father Christmas! They work in all areas of print advertising and TV commercials as well as music videos and corporate and training videos. Real people models can be any age, height, weight or ethnicity, depending on the product being advertised. These models must be good at expressing a variety of emotions so acting skills can help with this kind of work. Agents often require a selection of pictures representing a range of looks and expressions.

Speciality models

These models have something very different to offer. Some may have tattoos and body piercings from head to toe, some are dwarves, some are very fat, some pull amazing facial expressions and others can do weird things with their bodies! In fact, the more unusual the look, the better!

This type of modelling is very specialist so the amount you work depends on your particular look. Work includes advertising campaigns as well as television and film work.

Life modelling

These are artists' models who pose for an artist to paint, draw or sculpt from life. They can be male or female and are usually required to pose naked. Height, age and body weight depend on the requirements of the specific artist so this modelling is open to anyone who is able to sit still for long periods of time, and has a low embarrassment threshold!

Sports

These models have very fit, toned bodies and are usually very advanced at a particular sport. Many professional sports people, such as sprinters, rock climbers and swimmers, will join a sports agency to supplement their income.

There is also a lot of TV commercial work for these types of model, which can be very lucrative. You don't always have to be amazing at a sport to be photographed doing it, so this modelling is not restricted to professionals alone. If you are a model and have any sports skills you should always mention this when joining an agency as you never know what a client is looking for!

Walk-on and supporting artistes

Often referred to as 'extras', walk-on and supporting artistes appear in the background of TV shows, commercials and film scenes. They are essential in productions in order to build the shot and make it more realistic, adding a sense of character and atmosphere. For instance, a battle scene will need a number of soldiers, and a restaurant scene will need diners and waiters, all of which can be provided by the extras. They do not have individual speaking roles although they may be required to make background noise. There is no specific look required for this work although there is more demand for artistes between the ages of 20 and 40 and of average size.

To be a background artiste it is vital that you are patient and able to get on well with people. You are usually required to start very early in the morning, and days can be long with lots of waiting around (often on location in the cold!) This is not a short cut to get noticed as a TV or film star – if you want to be an actor you must go to drama school! It is, however, a good way to learn about the film and TV industries. Extra work can be great for providing regular income as you will often be booked for prolonged periods.

02 approaching an agency

approaching an agency

In the previous chapter we described the various types of modelling, and hopefully you have found an area that suits you. Once you have decided on your preferred area, the next step is to find an agency to represent you. Agencies, also called management companies, have a huge bank of contacts, and nurture relationships with a variety of clients, such as magazine editors, advertising agencies and clothing designers. It is crucial to your success that you sign up to a reputable agency as it is their job to develop your look, send you to castings and auditions with potential clients, negotiate fees on your behalf, and guide and develop each stage of your career. In return they will take a percentage of your earnings.

Before you begin approaching agencies, prepare yourself for rejection. Remember that not every agency is right for everyone and an agency will only take on those models they believe will be offered regular work. In fact, it is extremely unlikely that the first agency you approach will take you on; some of the most successful models were turned down numerous times before finding an agency to suit them.

Agencies employ model scouts who are always on the look-out for new talent. Agencies also have open calls at their offices, and their representatives regularly attend model conventions. Alternatively, you can send in photographs directly to your chosen agencies. In this chapter we will help you take those first steps to finding a good agent and help you embark on your model career.

Looking the part

The biggest mistake made by potential models approaching an agency is to wear too much make-up with over-styled hair and the latest fussy fashions. Obviously you want to look your best but an agent will notice you more the more natural you look.

Dress as simply as possible. You should show your body shape so wear nothing too baggy but also nothing too tight. Girls should wear jeans and a vest top with heels (a comfortable pair as you don't want to be tottering around unable to walk!). Boys should wear jeans, a T-shirt and shoes or trainers. Do not spend money on designer outfits; agents look for people who look great even in the simplest outfits.

Girls should ideally wear no make-up but if you must, then keep it simple with a little mascara, some concealer and a natural lip gloss. Agents want to see a blank canvas on which a make-up artist can create a look and will often ask you to remove your make-up if they feel you are wearing too much.

Hair should be clean, lightly styled and split end-free. Do not tie your hair back. An agent will want to see how it looks hanging naturally. If you want to colour your hair make sure it is done professionally and choose a natural looking colour. Ideally, however, it is best to leave it natural. Once an agency has signed you they will decide if you need to have your hair coloured or restyled. An agent will prefer shoulder length or long hair as this is more versatile to work with.

Scouting

This is the easiest (and luckiest) way to get into modelling. Many successful models were scouted, and this literally consists of an agency 'scout' approaching you on the street. This could happen anywhere, from shopping on a high street to having a coffee in your local café. For instance, Kate Moss was famously scouted at London's Heathrow airport!

This method relies to a great extent on luck and on being in the right place at the right time, but you must be realistic. If you live in the middle of nowhere, the chances are you will never be scouted. On the other hand if you live in a big city and have not been approached, chances are you are not right for modelling. Agents, photographers, make-up artists and stylists are always on the look out for new faces.

If you do get scouted make sure you do your homework. It is likely that if one agency wants you so will a few others, so it may not be wise to sign up too hastily. It is a good idea to look around and find an agency you are comfortable with.

Also be very wary of scam scouters. It is very flattering to be told you could be a model but do not let this impair your judgement. Never give them your telephone number. Instead, take their name and contact details and check on the internet that the company is legitimate before contacting them. Legitimate scouts and agents never ask for money up front. There will be fees for model cards and pictures but these will be deducted from your future earnings.

A scout is either paid a percentage of the agent's percentage from the model's earnings, or a set fee per model taken on by the agency. Therefore it is not in a scout's interest to approach anyone unless there is a good chance of success.

Sending or emailing pictures

Most modelling agencies have a section on their website for aspiring models stating their preferred method of contact. Most will ask you to send pictures either by post, email or via their website.

Any pictures you send should be good, clear snapshots: two head shots and one full-length, with minimal make-up and with hair down. Never spend money on expensive professional pictures before you get an agent. This is a waste of time and money; an agency can see what they need from a good clear snap, and want to see what you look like without make-up, professional lighting or retouching. If they take you on they will want to create a certain look for you.

TAKING GOOD SNAPSHOTS

A digital camera is preferable as this can be set to 'auto' and will deal with the focus, shutter release and aperture control for you. Ideally, the snaps should be taken outside in natural light with the flash turned off as the glare tends to flatten facial features.

Your head should fill the whole shot with your head positioned towards the top of the frame. Face the camera for one shot then turn sideways to show your profile in another. Keep you hairstyle simple and make sure your hair does not obscure your face. Full-length shots should look natural and not too posed. Turn the camera vertically so that you have a portrait shot and make sure your body fills the whole shot. Wear simple clothes that show off your figure; for women, jeans, a tight vest top and heels, for men jeans and a T-shirt.

Writing to an agency

Try to find out the name of the person you are writing to as this creates a good impression and your letter is less likely to fall by the wayside (it is perfectly acceptable to phone the agency to ask who this should be). Explain that you are interested in modelling and looking for agency representation. List your age, weight, eye and hair colour and measurements. For girls, state height, dress size, bust, waist and hips. Boys should list height, trouser and chest size.

Do not be tempted to lie as the agency will measure you if you are asked in for an interview and it could be very embarrassing! If you have any other skills, such as sports or languages (which can be useful for commercials), make sure you include these in your letter.

If you are sending photographs by post, clearly write your name and contact information on the back of each print in case the prints get separated from your covering letter.

If an agency is interested, you will be called in for an interview but if you don't hear back, chances are you are not right for them. Not all agencies will send a rejection letter. Agencies receive literally hundreds of requests every day from aspiring models, and will often only contact those they are interested in representing. If you include a stamped addressed envelope you will increase your chances of getting a reply. However, do not assume that just because they have requested to meet you they are going to take you on. It simply means that you have got through the first stage, which in itself is statistically very impressive! Make sure you are prepared for your interview. Research the agency so you know who their clients are and the models they represent. Turn up on time and be polite and friendly. An agency will use this meeting to see how you will come across to their clients.

model tip

TAKING MEASUREMENTS

- Bust: measure around the fullest part of your chest.

- Waist: measure around your belly button.

- Hips: measure around the fullest part of your bottom.

Walk in

This literally means walking into an agency at an open call time without the need to book an appointment. Make sure you do your research properly: check open call days and times on the agency website. Do not walk in at any other time, as the agency will not be happy! It is also a good idea to get in touch with the Association of Model Agents or equivalent in each country as they will be able to give you exact times and a list of reputable agencies and their contact details.

You will need to take snapshots with you and the agency will often take a few pictures of you there and then to see how you photograph and for their own reference. As previously mentioned wear simple clothes which show off your figure. Girls should have minimal make-up, wear their hair down, and wear tight fitting jeans and a simple vest top with heels. Boys should wear jeans and a T-shirt and no styling product in their hair.

Beauty pageants/competitions

Beauty pageants such as Miss World can be a great way of being noticed and getting exposure, as well as being a lot of fun. You can also win cash prizes, clothes and trips abroad and there are often opportunities to join agencies. Competitions in national magazines are also a good way to get noticed.

Be wary of competitions where you win a contract with an agency but have to use a particular photographer to take expensive professional photographs at your own cost before joining the agency. Remember, a legitimate agency will simply require a snapshot, not a professional picture.

Conventions

Model conventions are a good way for agents and scouts to meet hundreds of aspiring models in one or two days. Conventions vary greatly but usually include lectures on modelling, a catwalk show, an opportunity to meet agents and advice on hair and make-up.

Before you think of attending, check which agencies are going to be represented and the entrance fee. If it is local and you do not need to pay for hotels and travel, then it may be worthwhile, but otherwise it may be better to spend the money on going to see the agencies direct.

Model schools

Unlike doctors and teachers, models cannot simply be taught to model as it is a profession that depends to a large extent on genetics and physical characteristics. A good model school can however help you feel more comfortable in front of the camera and more confident around groups of people.

Be careful though as there are a lot of scam schools around making unrealistic promises to anyone who is willing to pay the fees. It would therefore pay to get feedback from former students before you decide to enrol. Beware also of model schools promising agency representation after attending one of their courses; this may not always be what it seems!

model tip

GENERAL TIPS

- Be punctual. An agency will see from this first meeting how professional you are.

- Be confident and do not feel intimidated by the row of glamorous model shots on the wall. Remember, they all started in the same position as you and it could be your picture up there in a few months' time!

- Wear figure-hugging clothes to show off the shape of your body. Keep your hair down and wear minimal make-up. The agency wants to see you as a blank canvas.

- Take a few snapshots with you: two head shots (front and profile) and one full length.

- Our personal recommendation is to send a couple of photographs to an agency by post or email, with a follow up call a few days later. If they want to see you they will arrange a specific appointment, and therefore have more quality time with you, and you will not have wasted time and effort on an unnecessary trip.

- Agencies in smaller cities are often much more relaxed about height and size requirements, so if you are unable to get into one of the major agencies, then you might try a smaller, more local one.

Which agency suits you?

If you find you are in the privileged position of having several offers from agencies it is important to do some research and determine which one suits your needs best. Firstly, check out the agency's reputation by asking for references. A legitimate agency will have no problem with you contacting their models and clients and will be happy to supply these details for you. Secondly, decide whether you want to be represented by a large or small agency. Bigger agencies tend to have better known models on their books and represent up to 200 female models alone. They will often have separate divisions for teens, new faces, high fashion, commercial and classic models. However, with smaller agencies these divisions will often be combined.

Larger agencies tend to have more bookers, clients and opportunities, and will attract the higher paid jobs. Therefore there will be more castings (the equivalent to auditions in the theatre world). However, there will also be more models competing for those jobs within the agency and often casting directors will ask each agency to send just a few of their models. With a larger agency it is important to find out how many models will be assigned to your booker besides you, and how much time and attention you will be given.

Smaller agencies often have only 20 or so models, and usually specialise in one or two types of modelling, such as sports models or men only. They are often well known within their speciality and have a few key clients.

It is your agency's duty to promote you to their clients and negotiate contracts on your behalf. In return they take commission ranging from 20 to 25% which comes from the work they have obtained for you. Remember, they work for you so carefully review the contract (this is your agreement outlining what the agency will do to earn the commission you will pay). Agencies usually try to represent a good range of models to fill the needs of their clients.

Questions to consider

Establish your competition within the agency. Are there other models who look similar to you? How much work do they get and does this mean the work will be shared? Another factor in deciding on your preferred agency is how well you get on with the bookers. Bookers are the point of contact between you and the client, so a level of trust and understanding is vital. Remember you will often be speaking to these people several times a day.

Consider your age. If you are a teenager for instance you may choose an agency that will be supportive in balancing both your career and your studies. Also with some agencies you may be put in the teen division whilst others put you straight into the main board – often depending on your look and talent rather than actual age.

The location of the agency. You will often be expected to go in to collect cards and refresh your portfolio, and some agencies expect their models to go in each day to collect the day's castings. Castings are also often held at your agency.

Can the agency help with accommodation? Some agencies have their own model flats. These are usually used by models from other countries but can be handy if you need somewhere for the short term. Beware though as the rent is often quite high, and although the agency will pay the initial rent for you, it comes out of your wages eventually! Flat sharing with other models can be fun as you have other people to go to castings with, but it can also be very cramped, often with three models in one room. It may also quickly become quite a competitive environment.

Does the agency have links with other agencies around the world? Thanks to the internet and ease of travel it is a lot easier for a model to establish a career all over the world. The main modelling areas are Japan, Hong Kong, Cape Town, Miami, New York, Paris and Milan. If you are keen to travel it is important to find out the agency's contacts and reputation worldwide.

How do they pay? You will need to find out whether you will be paid monthly, or whether you may get advances against future fees. In general, it often takes a couple of months for fees from a booking to be passed on to the model.

Discounts on hairdressers, grooming etc? It may be possible to get certain beauty treatments or hair styling at reduced rates through some agencies. Always check as you could save yourself quite a lot of money.

The level of commitment the agency expects from you? How easy is it to book out (take days off)? How many castings will you be expected to attend a day? Are you expected to pay to appear in their model book and website and how much will this cost you? How long is the term of contract? This will differ depending on the agency but it is usually one year.

model tips

- Be wary of internet agencies that charge high rates to display your pictures, and claim that top agents and clients frequently browse their sites to find new faces. In our experience no one has ever received work or indeed found an agent via this route!

- Do not get carried away by claims of high salaries. You may earn in an hour what you previously earned in a week, but remember that modelling work is irregular and not guaranteed.

- Be wary of a local agency claiming to be the biggest agency in the industry. Most bigger modelling jobs come from agencies in the cities.

- Get everything you are promised in writing and keep all your important documents, such as your contract, in a safe place. These will be needed should you ever need to take legal action.

- Interview your agent thoroughly. Remember, they are working for you, not the other way round, so do not let flattery cloud your judgement.

- Most legitimate agencies want a business name that is unique, so be wary of those whose names are purposely similar to well known agencies. Bogus agencies like to copy the reputable and established agencies to cause confusion and attract models and clients.

- Be wary of agencies that display pictures of famous models on their walls to make you believe they are represented by that agency.

- Never meet with a potential agent outside an office environment. Bogus agents have been known to invite potential models for an interview at hotels or bars to join an agency that doesn't exist. Once there the models are conned out of a registration fee and the 'agent' is never seen or heard from again.

- Listen to your agent's advice but in the end you must decide what is right for you. Some models do not want to travel the world or catwalk in front of lots of people, or be seen in underwear. Do what you feel comfortable with.

- If you are told by an agency that you are more commercial looking, do not feel offended as these models often earn a lot more money and can expect a much longer career than the average fashion model.

- If you think you have been scammed by an agency or model scout contact your local consumer protection agency.

03 working as a model

working as a model

Finding an agent is the first step to becoming a model but there are many more to climb before you find success. In this next chapter we will take you through portfolios, test shots, castings, what happens at a shoot, and what to expect on your first few jobs.

Getting the right exposure

YOUR PORTFOLIO

Your portfolio is your personal manifesto in the world of modelling. It is a book (or album) supplied by your agency containing a selection of pictures from test shoots and earlier work on advertising campaigns, as well as tearsheets from magazine work. This book is a model's most treasured possession and should contain the pictures that best 'sell' you as a model. When you go into a casting room it is largely from your book that the clients and casting directors will be able to assess your suitability for a particular job.

This is why it is preferable to feature a wide selection of looks in your book, appealing to a variety of markets. If your book contains as many different types of pictures of you as possible, the clients will have a better chance of finding what they are looking for.

Obviously you will want to focus on your strong points, depending on the type of modelling you do. However, you should also include a variety of shots, such as poses with other models or with children, in swimwear, or laughing, as well as some more serious show work. You can always take a picture out or or rearrange your portfolio depending on the casting you are going for. Open with a very strong head shot on your first page and finish on one of your best photographs, so leaving a good lasting impression.

Some models change their pictures frequently, depending on the casting. For instance, if you know the client is looking for a big cheesy smile you may substitute some of your more posed, serious shots for some happier ones. Alternatively you may choose to move these shots to the front of the book in order to make an immediate impact on the client at the casting.

It is advisable not to put too many images from the same shoot in your book. Always choose the best one or two and include just these to create the most impact. It can become boring for the clients if your book is too repetitive.

Think of your market and be careful not to confuse the casting directors. If the look required is very much girl- or boy-next-door, it is probably better not to include photos that are sexy. You should be constantly changing and updating your portfolio to reflect your improvement as a model, and also to maintain interest with casting directors, photographers and potential clients.

Although you will have spent some considerable time collecting and arranging your selection of shots, do not expect clients to spend very long examining each photograph individually. They see hundreds of books every day and will usually flick through quickly until one image stands out – and even then it is often just a brief glimpse. It can be very frustrating, but believe it or not that glimpse will often be all they need to book you for the job.

Sometimes at a casting there could be several members of the panel who are not engaged in browsing through your book, and it is worth taking this opportunity to ask about the shoot and the products to be advertised – you may also be able to find out exactly what look they have in mind. This will give you a chance to promote yourself and perhaps reference a photograph in your book where you have done a similar job. This will undoubtedly help them to remember you.

Never give any of your book pictures to clients at jobs or castings. If there is a particular picture they like they should call your agency for a copy. Your portfolio is your own responsibility, so make sure all the pictures are backed up on a computer or photocopied in case it gets lost or stolen. Never leave it out of your sight – this book is your main selling tool and your livelihood!

When you first start out you may have only one or two simple Polaroid shots in your portfolio, but some models

have won massive campaigns from such humble beginnings, so there is no need to be disheartened if your book is a little on the thin side! Like most things in life, it's all about quality, not quantity. Keep your portfolio fresh and updated with recent pictures; one way to achieve this is to arrange regular test shots.

TEST SHOTS

The easiest way to build up your portfolio when starting out is by means of test shots. This is a shoot set-up which is of benefit not only to the models but also to the photographers, stylists and make-up artists involved, all of whom welcome the opportunity to be creative and to build up their own portfolios. For this reason there is generally no fee for test shots, and more often than not the only cost incurred is the printing of any images you may select for your book. However, some photographers may charge a nominal fee, which may be worth paying in order to get some really professional photographs from a respected and established photographer. You may also have to pay a minimal fee to the make-up artist and for re-touching some of the shots. Your agent will be able to advise you on this.

Agencies will have their preferred test photographers and will often arrange tests on your behalf if they think more shots are required (you will need to check your own needs regularly with your booker). Most agencies have a queue of photographers who are keen to 'test' the models and so they will normally be able to recommend you to those most suitable for your book. Your agent will determine what types of look are missing from your portfolio, for example a body shot, strong head shot, an edgy fashion shot or a couple shot.

The photographer will get new shots and perhaps test out new styles of photography or try new lighting effects. The make-up artist, stylist and the model will all gain new photographs for their own portfolios. So it is in everyone's interest to get the best pictures possible. Generally, the better the photographer, the more likely they are to charge for the shoot. With free tests everyone stands to gain so you may not have much say in the end picture.

A test should be well thought out and everyone involved should know which shots are needed and which clothing is required to suit different looks. Some models choose not to pay for make-up and instead do their own, but we strongly advise you to use a professional, as it will almost certainly weaken the picture if you do not.

In some rare cases the test photography could produce a very strong shot, one that really stands out. This could lead to it being used in advertising and therefore a substantial fee for the model. If a photographer wants you to sign a model release form giving them permission to sell the shots, you should always check with your agent first. Some photographers agree a percentage that they will give you should the image sell. It has been known for models to be featured in big campaigns after testing with a photographer who loved working with them, and therefore produced some exceptional pictures.

CHOOSING THE RIGHT PHOTOGRAPHER

As with any profession, some photographers are better than others. A good photographer will have an in-depth understanding of lighting, background, ambience and posing, and they will find a connection with the model. Make sure you choose your photographer carefully. Do some research and look at their portfolio or website as this will give you a more accurate impression of the quality of their photography. Also look through fellow models' portfolios and ask who they recommend.

Make sure you ask the photographer about the copyright to the photographs. Check that you are allowed to have the negatives or the high-resolution files and that you are free to do what you please with them. Some photographers will sell the photographs to picture agencies who can then use them without your permission, so make sure you know where you stand when it comes to copyright, and if necessary agree on fees for any future sales.

COMPOSITE CARDS

These are a model's business cards and are designed to be left behind at castings or sent out to prospective clients for reference. They are A5 in size and generally comprise five pictures, usually a strong head shot on the front of the card and smaller pictures on the back. These test and work shots represent the model in as many different ways as possible: a full body shot, a couple shot, high fashion and girl- boy-next-door. Although a range is important, obviously if you are a sports model for example the shots will all be sporty, but will still include as wide a range as possible within that field. The card will contain the agency name and contact details so never leave your own personal contact details. Your agent will advise which pictures best promote you.

Only use strong shots on the card, as more often than not the client will decide who they will pick based on the composite cards. Make sure you show your personality and any exceptional attributes such as a great smile or amazing long legs. All good working models update their cards regularly. This is particularly important if you are travelling to different markets and if you change your look (hair or body shape). Ensuring your cards are fresh is the best way to keep potential clients interested. Some models even have two very different cards: perhaps one very fashion based and another more commercial, so they can select the more appropriate one for the job.

AGENCY WEBSITES

This is the main place an agency will advertise its models and it is essential you are represented on here. Agencies vary as to how many of your pictures they will put on their site. Some include your entire portfolio and some just select a few. It is essential that the pictures chosen are diverse to ensure a good range for clients. Most agencies charge you a fee for being on their website which will be deducted from future earnings, but this is minimal and simply covers costs.

MODEL BOOKS

Some agencies produce a model book which showcases pictures of all their models. This form of advertising is paid for by the model and it is usually reprinted every year. Many models resent having to pay for this as they feel the agency makes a lot of money from it, but thankfully, with the increasing popularity of the Internet, many agencies no longer produce model books.

Working as a model

THE CASTING

Castings (job interviews for models) are a chance for the client and photographer to meet you and look through your portfolio. Sometimes this may be a one-on-one meeting and at other times there could be as many as ten on the casting panel! As you walk in say hello and introduce yourself. Then hand them your book and wait until they ask you to sit down.

As they browse through your book this is a great chance for you to ask more about the shoot and what they are looking for in particular. Perhaps they want someone who is physically very flexible and you may be able to do the splits so tell them this! Try to provide as much positive information about yourself as this will help them remember you. Have a few answers ready to popularly asked questions, such as what work you have been doing recently. Try not to appear desperate as this will go against you.

Some castings are specifically for models the client has requested to see, but others are open castings, general castings or 'cattle calls', where the client has only a broad idea of the look they are seeking and invites anyone to come and cast for the job. These castings will often take a lot longer due to the number of models.

Castings may be held in a hired casting suite, the client's office, the photographer's studio, or at your agency. There is usually a waiting area where all the models wait their turn to

GILES

see the client. At this point you will put your name on the list and be allocated a number. There will often be a form to fill out asking for your agency contact details, measurements and recent work. Never leave your personal contact details.

Whilst you are waiting it is a great opportunity to catch up with other models, share experiences, compare books and get your own book in order. Make sure it is tidy with all the pictures neatly tucked into the pages, and that your model cards are nicely presented at the front of the book.

Your booker will give you times at which you will have to meet the clients for a casting. Sometimes this will be a specific slot, but on other occasions it will generally be between the hours of 10 am and 1 pm or between 2 and 4 pm. For specific times it is important to arrive punctually, and if it is a commercial casting, then try to arrive 15 minutes early to give yourself time to prepare, should there be any dialogue to learn. Commercial castings work in a very similar way to photographic castings: you will need to sign in and wait your turn to be called through.

Most agencies will request their models to 'check in' daily. This means phoning the agency between 4.30 and 6 pm to collect any castings for the following day. This is a very important part of being a model as you do not want to miss a crucial casting and it also reminds the agency not to forget about you!

WHAT TO WEAR

For commercial models this means dressing according to the casting brief. For instance, if the casting is for a corporate model assignment (for instance a bank) you may be expected to wear a suit. Although the client will have an idea of what they want to see from the various shots in your portfolio, it can certainly help to confirm your suitability if you dress in a way that fits in with what they are looking for. Obviously if you have several castings in a day it is not possible to dress for each so a simple vest top and jeans to show off your shape is preferable. Do not wear clothes that are unflattering or shapeless and avoid anything overly fussy or distracting with big logos.

As a fashion model it is important to have individuality, dressing to suit your body shape but still keeping up with the latest trends. One thing you will notice about most of the fashion models leaving a show is that they have lots of their own style but they all keep it simple. Looking good isn't about purchasing expensive designer labels, it's about style,

and style is always fashionable. The best way to keep up with the latest fashion trends is to look through glossy magazines and other relevant sources.

Getting the job

When a client wishes to book you for a job they will check your availability with your booker, who holds your diary. It is therefore essential to 'book out' if you are not available to work on a specific day. Otherwise an agency will assume you are free to work and book the job for you. If you have verbally agreed with the agency that you are available to work and then change your mind after the client has confirmed, you could be liable for any costs incurred – so be warned! Your booker will give you the following job details:

- Date and time
- Location
- Photographer's name
- Clothes and accessories required
- Whether you are doing your own hair and make-up
- Type of job and usage
- Fee

'Provisional bookings', 'options' and 'pencils' are expressions used if a client wants to book you provisionally for a job. These are not confirmed bookings and clients often option more than one model, but a model can take only one provisional booking. If another client wants to book you on the same day, they are given a 'second provisional' until the first client wishes to confirm. A 'pencil' is usually a lighter booking than an option or provisional so the job is not so likely.

ROLES ON A SHOOT

In most cases the client will hire an advertising agency which will then organise the photographer, photographer's assistant, models, make-up artist and stylist for the shoot.

The client has the final say over the finished picture, but it is the advertising agency that develops the concept for the shoot. On the day itself there will be an art director who will work closely with the photographer, make-up artist and stylist to achieve the planned shot. There may also be other representatives from the advertising agency there to assist.

The photographer will instruct the model during the shoot on how to pose, and the photographer's assistant will help the photographer with lights and the general set-up. Lunch and teas will usually be organised by the assistant or runner on a shoot. That said there are roles for everyone but they do slightly cross over and it is not unusual for all to chip in and work together.

It is important to not wander off to make a phone call or get some fresh air unless you know you are allowed to. Always make sure you stay informed about when you are needed. There will usually be a room in which you can relax where the client and photographer know where you will be. There is usually tea and coffee available as well as newspapers and magazines.

MAKE-UP

Unless otherwise informed by your agent you should always arrive for a job with a 'clean face' (meaning no make-up) and clean hair (with no use of hair gel or other products). Bring make-up with you in case the make-up artist does not have the correct products for you.

Men should be clean shaven. Take along some of your own hair products as the make-up artist may not have the right products for your hair type. For both men and women take deodorant and a toothbrush as you will be under hot lights all day and you may want to freshen up during the shoot.

Models often try to change their hair and make-up after a make-up artist has made them up because they think they know what suits them best. It is important to remember that as a model you are only a small part of the creative process, which could have been under consideration for weeks. The creative team know what is expected from the overall picture and have been hired because of their skills to achieve this. It is also boring if every picture in your book looks the same, so trust the team.

CLOTHING

If you are requested by your booker to take clothes on a job, you should take as many different types and varieties as possible. This may mean borrowing from friends and family. A case on wheels is ideal for transporting outfits. Clothes must be clean and ironed and displayed neatly in the changing room when you arrive at the studio. Unless bright colours are requested, neutral shades are usually preferred with no patterns or logos as the clothes should not clash with the product you are advertising. See page 18 for a detailed

list of garments you should bring with you to a shoot.

If you do not have one of the items of clothing requested for the shoot make sure you let your booker know so they can inform the client. You are not expected to have every type of clothing in every colour, so it is up to the client to find it in some cases.

Do not wear tight socks or bras that leave marks, and do wear flesh-coloured underwear (girls preferably a g-string) which can be worn under any type of clothing. 'Chicken fillets' to pad out your bra should be taken along too, just in case an outfit requires them.

Trips

This refers to an assignment where the model is required to stay away from home. It is usually centred on a specific outdoor location required for a particular shoot. A lot of catalogue clients shoot abroad for guaranteed weather, whether it be sun that is required, or snow for an outdoor clothing or ski-wear catalogue. On a trip the working day is subject to sunlight and often means very different working hours. For instance, the day may begin at 6 am when the sun rises and not finish until 7 pm, with a break between 2 and 4 pm when the sun is too high to shoot.

If you like to travel, trips are a great way to see the world. You will often stay in the best hotels, eat the best food and see the most beautiful places. All expenses are usually covered, including food, accommodation, travel and sometimes travel insurance but always check with your booker first to ensure that you understand fully what is involved. It is your responsibility to ensure you have a valid passport and make sure you inform your booker if you have any allergies or special dietary requirements.

Your booker will be sent an itinerary from the client listing the requirements for the shoot, including hotel details, travel arrangements, all contact details of those involved on the shoot and a list of any clothing that may be required. You may also need to have inoculations, depending on the countries to be visited.

Trips are also a great way to improve your portfolio. The locations will often be impressive and unusual, making your pictures unique, and they will look very impressive in your book. You may even be able to persuade the photographer to do a test should you need extra pictures.

Working on a trip is very much a team effort. Clients will want to take a model with an easy going but professional attitude, who is also prepared to muck in helping with bags and equipment. You must remember that this is not a holiday although everyone wants to enjoy themselves whilst still getting the best pictures possible. There will be drinks in the evening as everyone usually eats together, but remember you are there to work and look good, so avoid a hangover and bloodshot eyes.

Fashion shows

Fashion shows, also known as catwalk shows, are really the cornerstone of modelling as this is what the industry is most associated with.

Most models will say this is one of their favourite aspects of modelling, largely due to the fact that it is such fun; it's live, choreographed and you will have an audience applauding you as you walk the runway. The function of catwalk shows is to show off the clothes or products, so most catwalk shows require fittings to ensure the clothes fit you exactly.

You will usually work with a choreographer, often on the morning or the day before the show, who will instruct you where to stand, the timings at which you walk out and when to wear which clothes. A model can often have three or four changes and will have only seconds to change outfit so each model has their own dresser to help them. You will find that everyone changes in close proximity to one another so you cannot afford to be too self-conscious when doing a fashion show. There will also be stylists, make-up artists and floor managers all rushing around backstage to ensure the show proceeds smoothly. The key to the catwalk is confidence.

TV commercial shoots

These work in much the same way as a regular photo shoot, and the roles on the day are also similar, comprising the client, make-up artist and advertising agency. The main difference is that everything is shot on video or film, so a lot more people will be needed. These will include a director, producer, cameraman, assistants, runners, lighting people and electricians.

Every aspect of a TV commercial will have been very carefully planned, shot by shot, and this will have been agreed by the advertising agency and the producer. This is to limit cost and make sure nothing is left to chance on the day.

When you arrive on the set you will be told what is expected of you, and if you have any dialogue this will have been given to you in advance. You will be shown the storyboard so you know what you are expected to act out on the day, and you will be given all your call times. Be warned: almost always commercial shoots will run overtime, so it is advisable not to plan anything too definite for the evenings!

Make-up will differ from that used when working in a studio, as it tends to be stronger and more impacting in order to hold up to the bright lights.

A model's handbag

A model should always be prepared. You could easily get an unexpected last-minute casting or job whilst out, so it is vital to carry certain items with you at all times.

It is essential that your booker is able to contact you at any point during the day, so you will definitely need a mobile phone, and better still one from which you can retrieve emails. Make sure this is always fully charged and with you, because the day you leave it at home could be the day you miss out on the job of the year.

For girls, it is preferable to have two bags, a sports-style rucksack to carry your portfolio (often these are supplied by the agency) and a large shoulder bag that holds everything you need. Along with the usual paraphernalia you carry with you, make sure you always carry the following:

✓ Detailed streetmap. As a model this is your bible! Without it you will not be able to get to any castings or assignments!

✓ Mobile phone, so that your agency can contact you at all times.

✓ Diary, for writing down castings and jobs.

✓ Pen. It's amazing how many models forget to take a pen and get into a panic trying to borrow one to take down information from the agency!

✓ A model card. It's good to have one with you at all times as this is your business card.

✓ Book or magazine. It's an idea to have reading material with you as you will spend a lot of time travelling and waiting around on jobs and at castings.

✓ Make-up, mirror, hair brush, deodorant and tissues.

✓ Flesh-coloured knickers and bras, in case they are needed for a job.

✓ Safety pins – it's good to be prepared!

✓ Heels, to change into at castings.

✓ Health food bar, fruit, water and mints.

✓ Passport. You never know when you might have to jump on a plane to do a job.

The professional model

PERSONALITY

A pleasant personality is crucial if you are to become a successful model. Not only does it mean people want to work with you, but it will also show through in the photographs. You will be working with a wide variety of people from many different backgrounds, religions and sexual orientation, and it is important to have an open mind.

Whenever you meet people be polite, ask questions and make sure you integrate with the people you work with. Winning a job is often about perception: do they look the part? Do they seem reliable? Would I want to work with them? If the answers to all these questions are yes, then you're onto a very good start! Try to be as appealing in every aspect as possible.

Never forget how small the modelling industry is. Photographers, clients, stylists, agents and models all know each other, and if you are rude and difficult to work with you will find you will not get employment – there are many other models around to choose from. This is particularly true when it comes to assignments abroad. There may be five potential beautiful models at a casting but it will always be the happy, healthy, fun, relaxed model who will win the job. Clients do not want to spend a week working with a diva.

It's not always easy to be on great form when you could be feeling run down, hungry or tired. But try to be professional at all times.

PATIENCE

Patience is a virtue, and never more so than in the modelling industry! Waiting at castings, waiting to hear if you've got the job and waiting around endlessly on shoots… We strongly recommend you take a good book everywhere with you!

Make sure you use your free time constructively. Meet other models and look at their books for ideas, meet photographers and chase photographs from completed jobs. As in any business, success can only be achieved with hard work and dedication. The most successful models are those who see every day as a working day.

PUNCTUALITY

Turning up late for castings is very much frowned upon and reflects badly on yourself and your agency. The same applies for jobs; if you have a 9 am call time, make sure you arrive punctually (or better still 10 mins early).

If you do find you are delayed for some unavoidable reason, you should always phone your booker so that they can explain to the client on your behalf. If you cannot get hold of your booker, then your call sheet should have the name of a contact for the day, and you would need to call and warn them instead.

The best way to prepare for a shoot is to check out the location carefully on a map and plan your travel arrangements well in advance. Try to give yourself an extra 20 minutes leeway for any journey: trains can be delayed and it's better to be early and have a coffee than arrive late and flustered. If you are away on a trip always check the night before what time you will be expected to work in the morning. This is especially important if you are abroad as the call time will depend on the sunrise or the early light, so you cannot afford to be late – don't forget to check the time difference!

ETIQUETTE

As a model it is great to have a fun personality but you should not be disruptive on shoots or interfere with the creative team. If you are asked for your input, always be prepared to offer ideas but a gentle suggestion along the lines of 'how about trying it like this?' is likely to be welcomed more than any comments which might imply criticism. It is human nature not to like to be shown up!

If you are very experienced you will often feel you have a much better understanding than the client (or even the photographer on occasions) of how a shot should be approached, but it is usually best to just get on with the job. Usually it is recommended not to interfere with other roles unless asked. The client and photographer will have planned fairly intensively for what they want to achieve, so try to be as flexible as you can.

At times everyone may be so involved in their work that they forget all about breaking for lunch, while the model may be desperate for a sandwich! If this happens there is nothing wrong with requesting some time to eat – a banana or a health food bar can be handy standbys for times like these.

Dealing with rejection

For most, rejection is an unavoidable reality of modelling; the ups are amazing and the downs can be equally spectacular. There will be a lot of competition at each casting, and only one (or a few) will land the job, so you must learn to be philosophical. Accept that there will often be times when you are not selected, and do not see it as a personal rejection. Over the years we have learnt to simply go to the casting, be as friendly and professional as you can and then forget about it until you have a definite booking.

Try not to get too excited about being optioned or pencilled; although you are closer to getting the work this is in no way guaranteed. It is best to concentrate on the things you can control, like looking good, having the best book you can and doing a good job at the casting. No model is right for everything so try to stay positive.

Always remember that modelling is just a job. You may be flavour of the month and be working constantly, then simply because of a change in fashion, it seems that no-one wants to book you any more. More often than not this has nothing to do with you personally and is out of your hands completely. Competition from similar industries can also affect a model's career. Actors, singers, athletes and other celebrities are now competing for the advertising and editorial work previously reserved solely for models.

Model rights

As a model, you have the same health and safety rights as an employee in an office or a head of a company. All shoots must adhere to a code of practice and be insured against the possibility of something going wrong. This is normally down to the contractual agreement between the agency and client, and therefore not something you should worry about. The model rights also extend to your safety.

When a model agrees to undertake an assignment it is always under agreed terms, depending on whether it is for a poster campaign or for television advertising. It is up to the agency to agree a usage fee based on the size of the campaign (local, national or international) and the period of usage (e.g. one year). It is within your rights to be reimbursed should the company not honour the terms of the contract. Such instances would be for the agency to resolve, but always inform your agency if you see any work you have undertaken being used beyond the contractual agreement.

Your booker should explain the requirements for any assignment before you take on a job. If you are asked to do something you do not feel comfortable with during a shoot (such as nudity or kissing another model) which was not previously explained, it is well within your rights to refuse. Call your booker and they will advise you properly.

If a model is cancelled for a job with less than 24 hours' notice, they will receive a cancellation fee, and should the model cancel they will be liable for penalties too, depending on the circumstances. Always make sure you check your modelling contract.

Free time

You may have half days where you find you have finished your castings or a job by lunchtime, or days when you have no castings at all, so try to treat modelling as you would any 9-to-5 job and keep busy during your working day. Go to the gym, chase up completed work pictures and sort out test shoots to improve your book. Make sure your nails and hair are well kept and you are always well groomed.

As you are self employed try to keep on top of your finances. Keep a diary of which jobs you are doing each week and tick them off once you have been paid. Each night do a check list of everything you need to get done the following day. This will give you structure and motivation and keep you organised.

The benefits

PARTIES

In most big cities there are numerous bar and restaurant launches, award ceremonies, film premieres and parties, all of which require glamorous people. Quite often there is free food and drink and in some cases they may even send a car to pick you up.

The best parties are often during fashion weeks and over Christmas. As well as being lots of fun, these events are great for networking and meeting photographers and fashion designers.

FREEBIES

Freebies are not guaranteed from each job, however, as a model you are the perfect demographic for a lot of free products and services. Many clients feel that models stand out and with this association they feel their products will be noticed and their value will go up in the eyes of the general public. You can often expect to get heavily discounted or even free haircuts, grooming treatments, gym memberships, cosmetics, free meals and drinks, and clothing. Check with your agency to find out what is on offer.

04 the pose

the pose

Modelling isn't just about looking good and being photogenic; you also have to be able to change your pose according to the type of modelling you are doing. Ideally, you should alter your pose with every click of the shutter; small variations between each shot are all that is necessary, but it's important to keep the momentum going. Practise in front of a full-length mirror at home to get your posing down to a fine art.

Different types of posing

There are literally thousands of combinations when it comes to posing: edgy, cute, shy, serious, sexy – all of these expressions and more can be captured by working your body and facial expressions to fit the required brief.

FASHION POSES

Fashion editorial poses, for instance, are very different to catalogue poses. Fashion poses tend to be much more creative, with the model as important as the clothes in the overall picture, so the photographer and art director will be more involved with creating the poses. But it is up to you to convey the message of the picture, and your body language will reflect your state of mind and character. It is important, therefore, to determine with the photographer and client exactly what shot they are after, and pose accordingly.

CATALOGUE POSES

Catalogues shoots are done very quickly, with the model often modelling about 20 outfits a day, so the photographer expects you to have a selection of poses which best show off the outfit. The poses are only slightly different each time as they are all going to be used in the same catalogue and the focus is on the texture and fit of the clothing.

POSING WITH OTHER MODELS

This is one of the hardest parts of modelling, especially if you do not know the other model(s). Often you will be expected to act as if you are best friends, or even take up an intimate pose. If you are expected to do something unusual on the shoot like kissing or modelling underwear together, this will always be explained to you before you accept the job. Remember though, once you have agreed you must do what is asked. Forget your partner and what he or she might think – this is your job and you agreed to do the shoot. On the other hand you should never be pushed into doing something you are not comfortable with. Always call your booker if you feel uncomfortable, as it is their job to

sort this out; you should never have to feel pushed beyond your comfort zone.

It may seem strange but you have to learn to relax and to let go of your self image problems and focus on the job in question. Remember if you were booked for the job, you are the right person for it!

Another point to bear in mind is that the closer you are to the lens the larger you will appear. Girls should therefore stand alongside or slightly behind a male counterpart if they don't want to end up looking like a giant! Do not try to overshadow the other person – it is not all about you now!

Always wear deodorant and avoid eating spicy foods. There is nothing worse than spending the day doing close shots with someone who smells bad. It is easy (and relaxing) to start chatting when working with other models, but it is of paramount importance to remain professional and be alert to instructions from the photographer and client.

RED CARPET POSING

This must be the ultimate when it comes to posing, and you really are being viewed from every angle on the red carpet. As for any really important event you will want to look your best, and hair, make-up and clothes need to be immaculate. Only a small selection of photographs will be seen by the public, so give yourself the best possible chance by ensuring that every shot is a winner.

When being photographed on the red carpet, it's important to get in the right position. Women should stand either to the side or slightly to the back of a male partner. Never stand in front as you will dwarf your companion!

Designers welcome the opportunity to showcase their evening dresses, and often provide some of their most elegant and flattering designs for celebrities if this is likely to result in significant press coverage.

Most women on the red carpet put one hand on their hip, whilst bending the opposite knee, and combine this with a three-quarter pose. This is flattering because it tightens the skin on the upper arm, and the slight twist flattens the stomach, ensuring a flawless look from all angles. Stand tall, and remember to breathe in!

Alternatively you can put both hands on hips and stand with legs hip-width apart, throwing your weight onto one hip.

If you are wearing a backless dress, then the head over shoulder pose works really well. If you look closely at any celebrity magazine, you tend to find the same three poses being repeated. This is because they work!

Another tip is to smile with your eyes – any paparazzi photographer will say that the best pose is a natural smile. In fact paparazzi photographers use a brighter flash, which tends to flatten any lines or wrinkles on the face – an added bonus!

Men look better facing the camera directly as this projects an image of strength and confidence. They will often place one hand in a pocket, but only when the jacket is undone. Otherwise it is better to keep hands by your side with elbows slightly bent. Never place hands on hips as it tends to look effeminate. Legs should be a foot apart with one leg slightly turned outwards and the knee slightly bent. One hand will normally be in the trouser pocket of the straight leg, and the other hand should fall in the same direction as the bent leg. This hand should be relaxed – definitely no fists.

The aim is to look as relaxed as possible, so do not move too quickly as the paparazzi need time to get their shots. They will, however, take a succession of shots on motor speed in order to maximise their chances of capturing the perfect shot in the few seconds available.

If posing with someone else, always try to imagine the end result. Do you want to appear to be in love, just friends, the big star or just there for the fun? You also need to beware of cropping, as the paparazzi can create a false impression of a couple by conveniently cutting out others in the frame. Equally, if you want to appear with your partner as a couple, then it is wise not to give any unintentional opportunity for a news story by appearing too close to someone else, even if your own boyfriend or girlfriend is holding your hand. They can easily be edited out!

Most celebrities on the red carpet aim to stand out, and these events are an excellent opportunity to provide maximum exposure all over the world, via television news channels, newspapers and glossy magazines. Some celebrities have even been known to grow armpit hair (which is usually frowned upon) to ensure they receive greater coverage and many a red carpet appearance has helped to relaunch a failing career.

WEDDING POSES

Bridal wear fashion is big business. With countless magazines dedicated to the subject, there is always plenty of work available.

For obvious reasons, this type of work is dominated by female models, though there is some work available for men. Dresses are usually modelled on younger women, but brides come in all shapes, sizes and ages, so this type of modelling is open to most.

When on a shoot, think about the features you like about the dress and try to make them stand out in the shots. For instance, if you are wearing a backless dress it is a good idea to stand in the three-quarters pose, with your head over your shoulder. A more slinky dress gives more opportunity to show off your shape. Experiment with various poses, all the while thinking of how best to show the garment you are modelling.

Make sure you prepare for the elements: for instance on a windy day stand with your face to the wind so that the head dress and dress do not get blown across you. If it is raining, wait for the photographer to set up the shot before posing, and make sure you have an umbrella. If it is sunny, try not to look too much into the sun as your shots will result in squinting eyes. The photographer may want you to be in the full sun, in order to make use of the light. In this case, a good technique is to shut your eyes and ask the photographer to count down from three, then open them just as he takes the shot.

You should also consider where and how you hold your bouquet as it will cover some of the dress. If it is a princess-style dress, which draws in at the waist, it can make you appear larger if the bouquet covers the waist area. In this case the bouquet should be held either higher or lower than the waist.

Men should complement the bride by gently touching her waist and sometimes looking at her, and sometimes towards the camera. Standing three quarters to her tends to look better, and having one hand in the pocket can make you look more relaxed.

Remember your bridesmaids and groomsmen are there to help, so make sure they position the dress attractively, and also be alert to any problems that may occur.

For group shots, try to make sure everyone is doing a similar pose, whether this may be smiling together, laughing, serious or interacting with the bride. It is important to get a variety of shots, some fun and light-hearted, such as lifting the bride or throwing hats, and some sophisticated and elegant, such as formal posing. To ensure a good selection of pictures, aim for as much variety as possible, as this is hopefully a once in a lifetime experience.

POSING NUDE

Your agency will want to know whether you are happy to pose in the nude, topless or in lingerie and swimwear. This is completely up to you and you must only do what you feel comfortable with. If a job requires a model to be in lingerie or swimwear this will always be explained to your agent before you agree to the job, and so it should never be a surprise.

There is of course a big difference between nudity for a skin tone advertisement and nudity in a lads' magazine, so make sure your agent understands how you want to be marketed.

When shooting nude models, this is done on a closed set which means that only the vital members of the shoot are present, usually just the model, photographer and photographer's assistant. If you ever feel uncomfortable with what you are being asked to do, call your agent immediately, and if you feel anyone on the shoot is acting inappropriately, you should report them to your agent without delay.

Because of the job you do it is not possible to be shy and modest about your body. You will be changing in front of stylists, having make-up artists put make-up all over you, and at fashion shows the dressers may literally have to pull clothes off you.

Working your body

In most cases it is the model's responsibility to make the product they are modelling look good, whether it be clothes, a mobile phone or even a car. A skilled photographer will direct the model through different poses, but it is important to know what to do with every part of your body and to be aware your best and worst features and how to accentuate or hide these.

ARMS

Many newcomers to modelling are unsure about what to do with their arms. Should they rest either side of your body, should one arm be folded and the other not or should they be doing something more specific? The possibilities are endless of course but ultimately the pose you go for should be as fluid and as natural as possible, and should reflect the style of the product you are modelling.

For instance, arms folded indicates firmness and determination, and could be used for a powerful business shot demonstrating authority. The very same pose in a bikini or wedding dress, however, would indicate unapproachability, discomfort or even stress, and would not be appropriate for the product being modelled.

HANDS

Another big quandary when it comes to posing is what to do with your hands, and a lot of inexperienced models will have their hands clenched without even realising it! Props are a great way to overcome this – carrying a towel on the beach or holding a glass of wine for a party shot. When there are no props the most popular arrangement for hands is the 'catalogue' pose used in most catalogues. Here, the model relaxes the arms and holds her hands in front of her very loosely or barely touching. She can also use them to play with her hair, lean on, fold across her stomach or place on her hips.

Be careful not to cover either your face, the clothes or product with your hands or arms, and remember if your hands are too close to the lens they appear twice their normal size. Hands can look elegant near your face, but under the chin they can look like a growth, so be careful!

FACIAL AND BODY EXPRESSIONS

It is difficult to hold a natural expression for more than a couple of seconds, and usually a photographer will expect the model to move to a slightly different pose after each photo is taken. You will hear a click, and if they are using a flash you will see this go off, which is your cue to move. Sometimes the photographer will be using a very slow shutter speed and the pose must then be held for longer. If you are unsure you must always ask. Try to blink just before the shot is taken so your eyes are ready for the flash.

SMILING

Smiling on cue can be difficult, especially as there are so many different smiles – coy, happy, toothy, smug, proud. It's not always easy to look happy and natural when in front of bright lights and a crew of people, so it is worth taking the time at home to look at yourself in a mirror and practise. Try to cultivate a variety of different poses you feel comfortable with.

HEADSHOTS

When doing a headshot the photographer will position the lights for a close-up so it is important not to move around too much – just different expressions and subtle movements of the angle of your head are needed. Your eyes say a lot in a photograph and add warmth, sexiness or harshness. Many photographers will tell you to smile with your eyes. A good model knows their face. No face is symmetrical, so find your best side and work out what you want to accentuate or hide.

Holding your head tipped up slightly shortens the nose, accentuates the mouth and stretches out a double chin. Marilyn Monroe used to do this all the time. Dipping your head down gives an intimate expression and accentuates the eyes – this is not a good idea if you have a long nose, however. A three quarters view slims down a wide face.

Jewellery has to be photographed with the lights set up very precisely to capture the sparkle, so you may find that once in position you can hardly move at all, but at the same time you will be expected to look happy and relaxed in the picture!

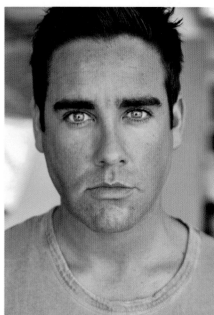

Walking

We often don't think about how we walk in everyday situations but walking graciously and elegantly is all part of a model's remit and it can be one of the most difficult aspects to master.

THE RUNWAY WALK

It is many a model's dream to walk the runways in Milan and Paris in the bright lights, buzzing atmosphere and glamorous clothes. But strutting your stuff with elegance and confidence takes a whole lot of practice and patience. There is no specific runway walk, as this tends to change with the fashions. Equally it is not the same as your usual walk along the street; it is a performance to show off the clothes to their best advantage.

Generally for girls the aim is to appear very graceful with lots of confidence, hips swaying, and looking forward, without smiling. For men, the clothes tend not to hang and flow in the same way as for women, so the walk is a lot more natural.

Remember you are being viewed and photographed from all angles so it is necessary to have an all-round good look and ease of movement. Confidence is vital and this comes primarily from practice. Stand straight and tall, keeping your shoulders back, and push your pelvis slightly forward. Never slouch. Relax your arms – there is nothing worse than arms stiffly hanging by your side. Equally, they should not be swinging around uncontrollably. Avoid walking with your hand on your hip as it can look staged. Hands and fingers should hang straight down.

Do not look down at your feet; keep your head straight, your chin up and look directly ahead. Your expression should reflect the clothes you are wearing and the designers will usually decide what is required.

At the end of the runway strike a pose. This is where the photographers are placed to get the best shots so hold your pose (this will depend on the show's choreography).

Enjoy yourself and as you become more confident you will find you develop your own signature walk with your own personality. Do listen to what is asked of you and never wave to the audience unless told otherwise. If you fall over or lose a skirt, just get up, laugh it off and walk on!

WALKING IN HEELS

When practising it is advisable to start with thicker-heeled stilettos with straps that cross the bridge of the foot to hold the foot in. It is best to have bare feet as you can feel every step and the sweat from the foot helps hold the shoe and foot together. One trick a lot of models use is to put double-sided sticky tape on the inside sole of the shoe so that your foot sticks to the sole – this works amazingy!

As you put each foot down, land first on the heel but instantly move the weight forward, not lifting the other foot until the weight has been correctly repositioned. The lower the heel the further back you should throw your weight. Imagine your hips doing a figure of eight moving forward before your feet.

A great way to learn this technique quickly is to practise in heels on a treadmill. This, however, may not be allowed at your local gym so you may have to resort to wearing high heels to the supermarket for your practice! You will need to know how to walk in heels on all surfaces – carpet, tarmac, marble cobblestones and stairs – so the more practice you get the better.

When going on public transport to castings, most models wear comfy pumps or flat shoes and then change into their heels at the casting or just outside. Otherwise your heels can end up feeling like cheese cutters!

Trial and error

It is very important to analyse and criticise your pictures, and constantly look for new ways to improve them. A good model will always be looking at poses in magazines for new ideas. Create a scrapbook of poses you would like to try out yourself from tearsheets from magazines so you can always refer back to them for ideas. Eventually you will become so comfortable that you will automatically select the appropriate pose for the shot and product. The best models are able to 'see' themselves from the outside when posing and know what the camera is capturing.

Courses in posing

Often photography courses and camera clubs require models to pose, and this is a great way to improve your posing without too much pressure. If you need a little extra help, there are also courses in posing, particularly for catwalk modelling. However, a good agency should offer its own instruction, so it is best to get registered with an agency before embarking on a course.

05 working abroad

working abroad

In order to further your modelling career and to improve as a model, you need to expand your skills. A good way of doing this is to take on assignments abroad. Working in new locations with new photographers and new clients will really help develop your career as well as provide some great new material for your book!

Model markets

Modelling markets differ from country to country; some countries focus on catalogue work, others on high fashion, with designers demonstrating their latest collections. In some countries the market is also seasonal. Cape Town and Miami for instance, are only operative for a few months each year, usually because of the weather. Cities like New York, London, Paris and Milan offer modelling work all year round but will be exceptionally busy during their respective fashion weeks.

Talk to your booker about the contacts they have with agencies abroad. They will have knowledge of the various model markets and will be able to advise you where you would best work. It is always better to have an agency that has referred you (your mother agency) as they will deal with your visas, immigration fees, tax and other such practicalities. Some agencies will front the money needed for initial living expenses and deduct it from your work pay. They will, however, take a percentage of your earnings.

All major cities have an element of modelling, with agencies of all sizes, although some countries suit some models better than others; for instant a western look is quite advantageous in Japan, whilst an Asian look may be sought after in South Africa. As you become more established as a model you will often book your year well in advance, knowing where to go and when. Initially, however, we recommend you plan to go for a short period of time. Two weeks is long enough to meet people and get a sense of the market.

Travelling the world can be fun and exciting, and working as a model is a great way to experience different cultures and earn money along the way. Remember, however, it can also be lonely and exhausting and you may not get to see your friends and family for months on end. Make sure you do your research before visiting and don't forget to take a travel guide!

Where and when to work

When arriving in a foreign country you should find out the general rules of what is and what isn't allowed and follow them. For instance, some Arabic countries expect women to cover up, and drinking alcohol in public in certain countries is illegal. In the United States, for instance, you are expected to tip taxi drivers and restaurant staff so always do your homework about the country before travelling.

ENGLAND (LONDON)

Modelling opportunities in London have greatly improved over the last few years, with world renowned British fashion designers making their mark and increasing credibility. Every type of modelling is covered in London, from supermodels to super sexy glamour models. The capital is highly popular with models the world over as the work is non-seasonal with a huge variety of clients and agents. Many TV commercials are shot here and there is also a lot of work in television and film. Editorial work in London is very edgy and modern so it is a great place to go to update your book.

ITALY (MILAN)

Milan is considered the 'capital of fashion'. A lot of high fashion originates here, from the very high profile fashion shows through to the fashion houses. Working here as a model is a great way to learn about the industry. Most of the major fashion designers and supermodels are based in Milan so it attracts models from all over the world. The general requirement is to be tall and slim. Very edgy and high fashion models work best in this market. Agents in Milan are likely to advance money to models who are just starting out. English is widely spoken and there is also a great transport system.

FRANCE (PARIS)

Paris is similar to Milan in the sense that a lot of big fashion houses are situated here. High fashion is what Paris is best known for, hence the term 'haute-couture'. It is a fantastic market for access to the high-fashion magazines and catwalk shows, although there is also some commercial work on offer. As with most big cities, living in Paris can be expensive so most models live in the suburbs where rents are lower.

GERMANY (HAMBURG AND BERLIN)

This is a great market and is mostly catalogue- and commercial-based. Models often stay in Paris and London and fly into Germany for work. It is a strong market for commercial models and can be very lucrative.

SPAIN (BARCELONA)

A lot of catalogue work is shot here as it is relatively cheap for other European markets to get access to year-round sun. It is a really exiting city and all types of models can do well here, although the market is mostly for glamour and commercial modelling.

GREECE (ATHENS)

Athens has long been considered a great place to develop your portfolio, as the landscape is so dramatic. Probably best between April and October as this market is very weather dependent. The downside is a lot of the work is less well paid, but you can get some fantastic pictures. Great for catalogue and magazine work.

IRELAND (DUBLIN)

Modelling in Dublin is growing each year with more and more clients moving there. The work is still mainly commercial although there are also a few high fashion campaigns. It is also very good for promotional-style modelling, and high profile models tend to become celebrities, doing press appearances, store openings, etc.

THE UNITED STATES

New York

There is a lot of modelling money to be made in New York. This is where the highest advertising rates are paid and the longest contracts given. There are a lot of fashion houses and influential designers here, so it is a very important market for modelling. New York is a year-round market offering a variety of work ranging from commercial/catalogue to high-fashion catwalks. A lot of the highest paying campaigns are booked from New York. Most of the best known brands advertised in magazines are also shot there. Living in New York is great fun with lots to do but it can also be hectic, with everyone rushing around, and it is easy to feel isolated. It is also an expensive place to live, especially Manhattan.

Miami

The work in Miami is very wide ranging, with everything from catalogue and sports to parts and glamour modelling. Due to the good weather and abundance of beach locations a lot of shoots take place outdoors and it is an appealing location for models and photographers alike.

Los Angeles

Los Angeles covers all types of modelling, with the majority being catalogue work. Like all major cities they have a fashion week, and also a large selection of model agencies. The work is mainly commercial with some access to major US campaigns. All in all a great place to work, especially if you are hoping to break into movies at the same time! It is a year-round market and a really fun place to spend some time.

JAPAN (TOKYO)

Japan is the heart of the Asian fashion industry. Modelling is generally catalogue- and commercial-based, and western looking models are very much in demand as the Japanese love western culture. Female models around 1.70 m (5 ft 7 in) tall and a clothes size 8 are preferred, as this best represents the Asian body type. Male models also tend to be slim to fit with Asian fashion.

Asian model agencies will usually draw up a contract for you, which covers a set period and a minimum earning figure based on the time of year and your look. In this way you are guaranteed to take something home when you leave. The amount can vary but as with any contract, do check how

much you will pay in commission and tax. The agent will also arrange accommodation, a driver and a guide.

The great thing about working in Asia is that modelling is given a lot of status, with some models describing their lifestyle as being similar to that of a rock star! Expect, though, to work harder than ever in Japan; the Japanese are known for being very meticulous. A knowledge of the language is definitely a bonus.

HONG KONG

This is almost entirely a catalogue market with many shoots being held here to cover the Asian territories. Many retailers and designers, as well as photographers and advertising agencies, base themselves here as it is a fast-paced city with many opportunities. The rates are very similar to those offered in Japan and models can expect to get very good contracts with guaranteed earnings at the end of their stay.

SINGAPORE

Singapore is a very commercial market so expect to do a lot of catalogue and magazine work here. Although it is not a massive market there is a lot of scope to work for neighbouring countries. A lot of models are on contracts here.

AUSTRALIA (SYDNEY)

This is one of the quieter modelling capitals. However, a lot of work for the Asian market also comes out of Sydney. The weather is fantastic which provides an excellent opportunity to shoot outdoors with natural light, and there is a varied landscape which makes for some very exciting photography. The work offered is mostly commercial/catalogue. It is not a massive market and you could find that there is a lot of competition, but Australia is a beautiful place and definitely worth a visit.

UNITED ARAB EMIRATES (DUBAI)

This is an emerging market and the gateway to the Middle East. As yet there are only a handful of agencies, but they offer some work for commercial models.

SOUTH AFRICA (CAPE TOWN)

Cape Town is a very seasonal market and the high season is from November to April. Lots of photographers and clients head over there for guaranteed sunshine, but also because it is cheaper, owing to favourable exchange rates and a reasonable standard of living. Lots of catalogues and commercials are shot here, but it is also a very competitive market for models.

Fashion weeks

Any country in the world that has a fashion industry will have a fashion week. This is when designers get the chance to show off their new collections to suppliers and the press. Los Angeles, Singapore, Hong Kong, Dubai, Cape Town, Sydney and Miami all have fashion weeks, but they do not tend to be so well covered in the worldwide press as the more well known ones in London, Paris, Milan and New York.

The legalities

Professional modelling agencies protect their corporate clients by assuring them that the models they represent are legally allowed to work abroad. Your agency will let you know exactly what you will need to do to obtain the correct documentation. You will usually need several tearsheets to prove you work as a model and often you will need to have a minimum amount of money in the bank, as well as relevant insurance documents, a passport and a social security number. If you do not have the necessary paperwork, you risk permanent exclusion from the host country and will not receive payment for any outstanding work, so make sure you resolve any legal matters before you travel.

Other restrictions for modelling generally involve lower age limits, with different countries stipulating various age limits for models in the industry. For instance, in Britain girls under the age of 16 are not allowed to work on the catwalks. In other (more extreme) cases models may have to prove that they are 100 per cent fit and healthy with documentation from their doctors to that effect.

Visas

A visa is the term used to describe your invitation to a country that is not your country of residence. There are lots of different types of visa: from student and temporary short-stay visas to permanent working visas. If you are modelling most countries require a work visa to work on their shores. These can vary in cost and length of time to obtain (sometimes between three and five months!).

All major capitals have embassies to represent their own country in a foreign land. Once you have established where

you will be visiting you will have to collect your visas from the relevant embassies in your country of residence. Always plan this in advance as there will be a lot of detailed information required, ranging from passport photographs to signed documents from agencies or previous employer references to validate you. Remember as well that should any problems arise whilst visiting or working in a foreign country the embassy will be able to help.

The legal documentation required to work abroad differs from country to country but below is an example of what it takes to qualify for an H-1B3 visa needed to work as a model in the United States.

H-1B3 fashion model visa

Any model wanting to work in the United States will need to be in possession of the correct documentation. The H-1B3 visa allows non-American fashion models to legally work in the United States. Your US employer (i.e. US-based model agency) will have to file a petition and will need you to provide a required set of documents to certify that you are a fashion model. Copies of tearsheets, newspaper articles and modelling contracts, along with other reliable evidence will all need to be made available. You will also need to prove that you have been sponsored by a fashion agency in the US. A filing fee (in addition to legal costs) in the region of US$1,000 will need to be covered by you. The American government will only authorise a certain number of visas each year and once they have been allocated they will no longer accept any further applications.

grooming

grooming

Healthy living is the key to being a successful model. A natural healthy glow is vital to modelling, and excessive dieting, drug use and too much alcohol will ruin your looks prematurely and you will not get work. You must be careful what you eat but the emphasis must lie with healthy eating and not drastic dieting. It is not possible to starve yourself and still have beautiful skin, hair and nails. Health is more than just about your weight; it is about the quality of the food you eat and your fitness levels.

Diet

Food is like fuel to our bodies. The body needs a balanced mix of nutrients in order to function properly. A poor diet can lead to ill health, and though the signs may not be immediately apparent, you run the risk of suffering from brittle bones, weak nails, bad complexion, dry, lanky hair, depression, low energy levels, heart disease and general poor health.

A healthy diet should include a balance of fresh fruit and vegetables, wholemeal bread, fish, lean meat and plenty of water. Where appropriate, food should be steamed or grilled and fatty foods and dressings should be kept to a minimum. To maintain a healthy body weight women should consume around 1,800 calories per day and men 2,200, including alcohol. Both men and women should drink between 1.5 and 2 litres of water a day to avoid the symptoms of dehydration, which include headaches, loss of concentration and tiredness. Include the following foods in your diet to ensure your body functions to its optimum capacity.

FISH AND MEAT

Try to have at least two portions of fish a week, including one of oily fish. White fish, such as haddock, cod, sole and plaice, are low in fat; oily fish, such as tuna, mackerel, salmon, trout and herring are all rich in omega 3 oils. Fish is an excellent source of vitamins, protein and minerals, and is great for healthy skin. Grill, poach or bake fish and avoid fried fish and fish in batter.

A grilled or roasted lean pork chop, rump steak, or chicken and turkey breast (skin removed) makes a delicious meal alongside a bowl of salad. Go for the leanest option and trim off any excess fat. Avoid burgers, sausages, salami and meat in pastry as these tend to be very high in fat, and the best cuts are rarely used.

DAIRY PRODUCTS AND EGGS

Dairy products are an excellent source of protein, calcium and vitamins, but remember they can often be high in fat. Opt for skimmed milk, low fat fromage frais, cottage cheese and natural yoghurts, and avoid full fat rich cheeses such as Cheddar and goat's cheese. If you do have them, have them in moderation!

Eggs are fantastic for providing protein and energy. Try to buy the organic or free range variety. Boiled or poached eggs are less fattening than fried or scrambled eggs, and soft-boiled eggs with wholemeal toast is a great way to start the day, as are omelettes made with egg whites as they contain less fat. Don't overdose on eggs though as they are high in cholesterol.

FRUIT, VEGETABLES, GRAINS AND NUTS

Fruit and vegetables are high in fibre, vitamins, minerals and all good nutrients. You should aim to have at least five portions of fresh fruit and vegetables a day. Only buy fresh and wherever possible organic. Avoid fruit bars that are high in sugar and tinned fruits as these are high in sugar and sweeteners. Dried fruit, such as apricots, prunes and dates are great for snacking on.

Starchy foods such as bread, cereals, rice and pasta are an important part of a healthy diet and should make up a third of your food intake. Go for the wholemeal varieties as these are a great source of energy and will also help with digestion.

Eat nuts in moderation and avoid salted or roasted nuts as these are high in salt and fats. Nuts make the perfect snack for models on the move as they are high in fibre and nutrients as they are easy to carry with you.

TINNED FOODS

Tinned beans are a great source of nutrients and fibre. Avoid tinned beans with added sugar, salt or preservatives. Tinned baked beans, butter beans, kidney beans and chickpeas provide bulk, are a great source of protein and are perfect for vegetarians.

FLUIDS

Are you getting enough fluids? Dehydration affects your skin, sleep and weight so it is vital to drink between 1.5 and 2 litres of water a day. If you are exercising a lot or are in a hot climate, you should aim to up your water intake.

Wherever possible drink water, natural fruit juices and herbal teas. This will keep your system hydrated and your body working to its optimum capacity. Alcohol, coffee, tea, high-sugar and fizzy drinks, and sweetened juices should be avoided.

diets

We have found that the best way to stick to a diet is to eat healthily during the week but allow yourself one naughty day over the weekend to eat what you like. You will probably find that it is hard to diet on shoots as most clients want easy food for lunch so will order in pizza or sandwiches and crisps. Do not feel embarrassed to take your own healthy lunches with you though!

Exercise

Exercise is a great fat buster! If you can afford it, join a gym. It's a worthwhile expense and will not only keep you fit but mentally active. Gyms are great on days off to keep you disciplined and it is good to have somewhere to go that is familiar. Alternatively, go jogging, hiking, walking or follow a DVD exercise routine that you enjoy. Yoga, pilates, step, dance… the possibilities are endless! Do whatever works for you and try to keep your routine varied so that you don't get bored. You should aim to exercise regularly, about three to four times a week.

If you are working away from home or don't have easy access to a gym, the following exercise plan provides a great home workout. Designed as a complete all-rounder to help you achieve a lean and toned figure, the programme is broken down into sections to work specific parts of your body. This exercise routine will keep you lean and fit without increasing your body mass. All you need is an exercise mat, loose clothing, a good pair of trainers and an Exertube.

Remember to stretch after the routine to reduce any aching. Older models should consult their doctor before doing these exercises; often, simple stretching exercises are preferred. Repeat the full workout if you are feeling particularly energetic but this is a good workout to do three times a week.

JOGGING ON THE SPOT

Jogging on the spot is a great warm-up before you embark on your exercise routine.

① **Stand with your feet hip-width apart and jog on the spot. Don't bring your knees up too high, and keep your upper body relaxed and arms slightly bent as if running. Do this for about 5 minutes.**

SQUATS

Squatting will warm up the lower body muscle groups and tone your thighs and bottom.

① **Stand with your feet shoulder-width apart and knees slightly bent so your knees aren't locked with your hands placed on your hips.**

② **Bend your knees 90 degrees with your body leaning slightly forward until it is at a right angle to your thighs and keep your heels firmly to the floor; do not lift them and make sure you keep your back straight. Repeat 25 times.**

BOTTOM AND BACK OF LEGS WORK-OUT

This is great for your bottom and the backs of your legs.

① Lie on your back with your feet flat on the floor and about 30 cm (12 in) distance from your body. Your arms should be at your sides with your palms facing down.

② Lift your hips until your legs form a straight line with your upper body. Tense your bottom and pull your stomach in tight, then slowly lower to the start position. Repeat 25 times.

LUNGES

Lunges are great for sculpting your thighs and bottom.

① **Stand with your feet shoulder-width apart with hands on your hips.**

② **Keeping your upper body straight, step your right leg forward. Now bend your right leg so that your knee is directly above your foot. Lower so that your left leg is bent 15 cm (6 in) off the ground.**

③ **Now push up with your right leg and return to the start position. This should be done in a controlled manner for 2 to 3 seconds. Swap legs and repeat 30 times for each leg.**

BUM KICK BACKS

Ideal for toning and shaping your bottom.

① **Kneel on all fours with your knees, elbows and forearms touching the floor, and hold your stomach in tight.**

② **Now kick one leg directly back so that it is in line with your body. Do 25 repetitions on one leg and 25 on the other.**

JOGGING ON THE SPOT

Now jog on the spot to get rid of any lactic acid build-up and to get your heart rate up. The faster you jog on the spot the more calories you will burn. Try to aim for a burst of 60 seconds. As you get fitter increase the tempo.

TRICEP DIPS

Tricep dips are perfect for toning the backs of your arms.

① **You'll need a sturdy chair or the edge of a table or bed. Face away from the object and walk your legs to about 60 cm (2 ft) in front of you. Now with your hands behind your back and palms down find the edge of the object; your arms should be shoulder-width apart and keep your elbows in. Now start to lower your body.**

② **Keep your body as close as possible to the object by lowering your body so that your arms are at a 90 degree angle and slowly push up your body. Repeat 15 to 20 times.**

PRESS-UPS

Define your shoulders and chest with a series of press-ups.

① Lay flat on your front with palms to the floor and arms shoulder-width apart in line with your shoulders. Your legs should be in line with your hands.

② Now push yourself up, trying to keep your body as straight as possible. Lower yourself back down, bending your arms without letting your body touch the floor. Keep your body in full tension, then repeat slowly 15 to 20 times. If this gets too difficult do half press-ups; here your knees and toes remain on the floor at all times.

SHOULDER PRESSES

This exercise will define you deltoids and other shoulder muscles.

① **Place the Exertube firmly beneath your feet and hold it behind your arm with your elbow bent at a 90 degree angle and clench your stomach.**

② **Lift your arm straight without locking the elbow and exhale as you do. Breathe in as you lower to the start position. Repeat 30 times on each arm.**

SIDE RAISES

Another great exercise for shoulders
and also for improving your posture.

① **Place the Exertube beneath your feet (to increase the difficulty place your feet slightly apart to increase tension on the band). Keep the handles of the tube by your sides and your arms straight but for a slight bend in the elbows.**

② **Raise your arms to your sides at a 90 degree angle. Now slowly lower them back to the start position, making sure you don't swing from your arms. Keep your posture straight and your stomach in. Repeat slowly, 15 to 20 times.**

BICEP CURLS

Tone the front of your upper arms and tighten your forearms with these bicep curls.

 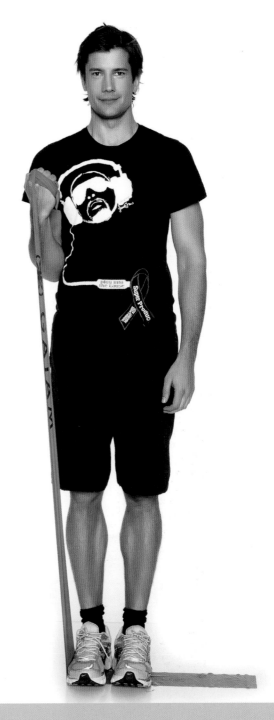

① **Place the Exertube beneath your feet (to increase the difficulty place your feet slightly apart to increase tension on the band). Keep the handles of the tube by your sides and your arms straight but for a slight bend in the elbows.**

② **Alternately raise your forearms so that your hand touches your shoulder. Now slowly lower back down to your side, making sure you don't swing from your arms. Keep your posture straight and your stomach in. Repeat slowly, 30 to 50 times.**

SKIPPING ON THE SPOT

This is great for working your legs and upper body, and for raising your metabolic and heart rates.

① Stand with your feet together, posture straight and stomach in. Start with the skipping rope behind your heels.

② Now whip the rope over your head and jump a little off the floor. Continue for 1 to 2 minutes. If you don't have a skipping rope, just jump on the spot to simulate a skipping rope jump.

STOMACH CRUNCHES
The name of this exercise says it all!

① Lie on your back on an exercise mat and lift your knees so that they are at 90 degrees to your body and keep your back flat to the floor, making sure you do not arch it. Put your hands to your ears.

② Slowly and in a controlled manner, lift your shoulders off the floor and bring your knees slightly toward your head. Return to the start position, taking a few seconds on each to get the perfect stomach crunch. Repeat 20 to 50 times.

OBLIQUES

Obliques are ideal for ironing out any love handles!

① Lie on your back on an exercise mat and lift your knees so that they are at 90 degrees to your body and keep your back flat to the floor, making sure you do not arch it. Put your hands to your ears.

② Keeping your right foot firmly to the floor, lift your shoulders and point your right elbow as close as possible to your left knee, then lower slowly back to the floor. Repeat on the opposite side. Do 20 to 50 repetitions.

LOWER BACK EXTENSIONS

Great for supporting and strengthening your lower back.

① Lie on your front on an exercise mat. Bring your hands to your ears and point your toes to the floor.

② Using your lower back muscles, Raise your upper body 20 cm (8 in) off the floor. Hold for a beat and then lower. Try to use only your lower back muscles so as not to place unnecessary strain on your neck. Repeat 20 to 30 times.

LOWER STOMACH

These are great to define the V in your lower stomach and strengthen your core stomach muscles.

① **Lie on your back on an exercise mat with your lower back flat to the floor and stomach pulled in tight. Lift your legs towards the ceiling.**

② **Pull your lower stomach muscles in tight and raise your bottom off the floor, pulling your legs slightly in towards you. Hold for a beat and return to the start position. Repeat 15 to 25 times.**

RUNNING STEPS

Great for toning legs and raising your heart rate.

① **Find a step or a ledge with enough grip. Place one foot on the ledge, then the other, as if you were walking up a flight of stairs. Repeat 40 to 60 times.**

Sleep

Some people think that modelling is about endless celebrity parties and late-night clubbing, and although your social life will likely be rather hectic, it is important to make sure you get enough rest. You should have about eight hours' sleep a night. A good night's sleep is vital to looking your best, and a model with bags under the eyes and a hangover will not be booked for jobs. Even with the best make-up artist, poor, tired skin cannot be concealed and clients will simply book another model rather than pay for expensive retouching.

Skincare

Good skincare is important for both men and women, and we strongly recommend a professional salon facial every six weeks to purify and detox the skin.

Many factors affect the health of your skin, including pollution, poor diet, stress, age and hormones. There is, however, lots you can do to improve the look and feel of your skin. Water is essential for keeping skin hydrated and eliminating toxins, so make sure you drink between 1.5 and 2 litres of water every day. Include lots of fibre in your diet, along with plenty of fresh fruit and vegetables. Good fats are vital for healthy skin and are found in wholegrains, seeds, nuts and oily fish. Finally, nutritional supplements give your system a boost – multivitamins and minerals can be taken but should not be taken in place of a balanced, healthy diet.

Start your day with a mini cleanse and detox by drinking a glass of hot water with a squeeze of fresh lemon. Avoid too much caffeine and alcohol as these drain moisture from your body.

Apply a honey facemask for 30 minutes and rinse off with warm water. This will leave your skin looking soft, subtle and nourished. Apply three times a week.

Acne

Although acne is more common in teenagers, many adults suffer from it too. It is often due to a hormonal imbalance, but more often than not it is down to a poor diet. One obvious way to help keep this complaint under control is to drink lots of water to flush away toxins and to eat plenty of fresh vegetables, in particular carrots, lettuce, watercress, celery, dandelion leaves and nettle leaf infusions. You can also take nutritional supplements, such as vitamins A and B, zinc and borage oil; there are lots of natural remedies, so check with your pharmacist. Bathing or steaming the skin with a few drops of tea tree oil or camomile helps clear pores and gives your skin a healthy glow. There are, of course, medicines available on prescription so consult your doctor.

Stretch marks

A high percentage of women suffer from stretch marks. These unsightly reddish steaks can be found around the breasts, thighs and abdomen. They do fade slightly over time but will eventually turn into thin white scars. Stretch marks usually appear after excessive weight gain or loss, pregnancy or due to a deficiency in zinc. Though they are less common in men, they can also suffer from them and they are caused by rapid weight loss or gain, or a notable decrease in muscle mass.

Swimming, dancing and stretching can help reduce stretch marks, and homeopathic tissue cell salts such as silica help keep cell tissue firm and elastic. You can also take vitamins B5 and C, and nourishing vitamin E cream or oil to rub onto the skin. There are also many anti-stretch mark creams available but these can be quite expensive so make sure you look into these carefully before buying.

Tanning

Almost everyone looks better with a tan! A tan makes you look healthy, improves the appearance of your skin and can even make you appear slimmer! You should, however, aim to achieve a healthy glow and tanning should not be taken to excess – there is nothing worse than orange skin!

The dangers of excessive sunbathing are endless, so fake tan makes a good, safe alternative. There are many fake tan products on the market so find one that suits you best. Ask friends for their recommendations and do your research as some products are better than others. Always exfoliate thoroughly before applying tanning lotion and do not wear deodorant as this can stain the skin green! Be especially careful when applying to knees, ankles and elbows as these areas are prone to streaking.

Ideally wear plastic or rubber gloves when applying fake tan, otherwise wash your hands immediately afterwards. Always apply at night before bedtime and wash off in the shower in the morning. If you find you have streaks, rub off with a little nail varnish remover on a cotton wool pad.

Airbrush tanning is also very popular and is done in salons. This tan is sprayed onto your body in a fine mist and works with the amino acids in your skin to cause a chemical reaction. Always exfoliate first but do not apply moisturiser straight afterwards.

Wear old clothes as the tan will rub off onto them although it does wash out. Clothes should also be loose to avoid marks, and flip flops are recommended. This tan can look very dark before it is washed off and should be left on for at least eight hours. We therefore recommend you do this in the evening and wash it off in the morning. Some spray tans are so natural you look as if you have just returned from a two-week holiday in the sun!

If you do wish to tan naturally always wear a high factor sun protector, which contains UVA and UVB filters to shield your skin from ultraviolet radiation. Avoid tan lines as these will show up in photographs.

If you are working in the sun for prolonged periods make sure your skin tone stays the same. It can be very appealing to sit in the sun between shots but you must be very careful not to get tan lines or change colour dramatically as this will ruin the shoot. Many clients do not allow models to sit in the sun for this very reason. Also ensure you wear a protective moisturiser on your face before make-up is applied as you will burn through the make-up. And always wear sunglasses to avoid premature lines around the eyes caused by squinting!

Dry skin/peeling

This can be caused by lack of hydration, poor diet, too much alcohol or lack of sleep, but in many cases by exposure to too much sun! The best way to avoid dry, scaly skin is to moisturise after your morning or gym shower and before you go to bed. You don't have to spend a lot on a good body moisturiser but look for one that contains vitamin E as this helps prevent peeling. Use a good quality moisturiser on your face as the skin is a lot finer and more sensitive, and take particular care when applying cream to the eye area as it is very delicate.

Make-up

Try not to wear make-up when you are not working as it's important to give your skin a break. If you take good care of your skin you should need little more than a dab of lip gloss and a coat of mascara for day wear. There are, however, a few tricks of the trade that professional make-up artists use to highlight your best assets. You may also find on some jobs that you are asked to do your own hair and make-up so it's important to have a good all-round knowledge on grooming.

FOUNDATION

Choosing the wrong colour foundation is one of the biggest mistakes made by both women and men. It is very important to find a foundation that blends in with your natural skin colour, so always check the colour in natural light before buying. It should not feel or look like a mask. It is a good idea to buy a foundation with a sun protection factor as it will ensure your skin is protected throughout the day. Use a concealer to cover up blemishes and dark shadows under the eyes, and a foundation as a light base for the rest of your face. Most make-up artists suggest applying a good moisturiser and then a non-oily foundation, or even blending the two together before applying. To finish, brush a light dusting of loose powder over your face.

EYELASHES

An eyelash curler is a great tool to open up your eyes and is suitable for both men and women. This should be used before mascara is applied. Use a good mascara that thickens and lengthens the lashes, but make sure they do not end up looking clumpy. To ensure natural looking lashes, run a clean eyelash brush through the lashes after mascara application. Mascara is sometimes used on men for shoots though we do not recommend its use at any other time. A clear mascara, however, can look natural and is a good way to emphasise your eyes.

EYEBROWS

These are possibly your most important feature as they frame your eyes. It is easy to over-pluck so women should get this done professionally. Threading – using twisted cotton thread to pull out the hairs – not only gives a good finish but also thins the hairs over time. Waxing lasts longer than plucking but it is hard to achieve a perfect shape. Electrolysis will permanently remove the hairs but should only be done on the strays as you don't want to remove too many and regret it! Always use a brow brush to keep your brows tidy.

For men it is important to keep a check on any unruly hairs. Buy yourself some good quality tweezers and pluck the hair in the middle of the brows and a little above the brows. The key is not to over-pluck as it will look too feminine.

NAILS

Both finger- and toenails should be well manicured as these are a big part of your overall presentation. Fingernails should be kept neat, not too long, and oval in shape for a natural look. Girls should wear clear or French varnish; if clients want a different colour they will let you know or advise the make-up artist. Men should keep nails clipped back neatly and certainly not bitten or too long.

TEETH

Recent years have seen an increase in cosmetic teeth whitening. This is a quick and effective way to give your teeth a new lease of life and can be performed at most dental surgeries. As a model it is important to have clean white teeth but just as important for them not to look too white; they must still look natural in pictures.

Strong, healthy teeth require calcium which can be obtained from sesame seeds, chick peas, dairy products and figs. Most vegetables and wholegrains also contain vital minerals for teeth.

Make sure you brush your teeth gently after each meal, floss every day and rinse with a natural mouthwash. It is a good to take a toothbrush on shoots to keep your teeth clean after lunch. Some models use petroleum jelly on their teeth to stop their lips from sticking when they smile and to give a brighter smile as substance reflects the light.

To maintain healthy teeth have regular checkups with your dentist, orthodontist and hygienist. If you need braces this will not stop your modelling potential and is a short-term solution to a long-term smile.

FACIAL HAIR/STUBBLE

It is important that your face looks groomed at all times. This is essential when meeting prospective clients for the first time or when you are on a job. Some male models look better with a light stubble while others suit a smooth look. It is all subjective of course; the key is no matter what your style is, make sure it looks well groomed!

The best time for men to shave is when the skin on the face is at its softest, either straight after a hot bath or shower. Use a facial exfoliator to lift the hairs, then apply shaving foam, oil or cream. Massage into the skin and leave to soak in for a few minutes, shave and then rinse off with warm water. Finally apply cold water to the face to close the pores. Make sure you replenish your shaver every seven to 10 shaves.

HAIR REMOVAL FOR GIRLS

Shaving is quick and easy but doesn't last very long. Although waxing can be painful it is the best method of female hair removal. It gives a smooth, soft finish, lasts longer than shaving and ensures much finer hair re-growth. Always get waxing done by a professional to avoid bruising and unnecessary discomfort.

Always exfoliate a couple of days before waxing as it frees any hairs trapped beneath the surface of the skin and ensures the hair is pulled from the roots. Allow a couple of days for the skin to recover as it can be red and sore and you certainly won't want to be doing an underwear or swimwear shoot the next day.

Bikini line: this should be waxed every two to three weeks. Never shave this area as it will encourage in-growing hairs and cause a nasty rash.

Under arms: either wax every two to three weeks or shave every day. You will find re-growth will be faster in the summer as you sweat more.

Legs: wax every three to four weeks or shave every other day.

Lip hair: wax once a month or invest in electrolysis. Bleaching is not advisable as although as the hairs may appear lighter, they are still there! Do not be tempted to pluck this area as the hairs will grow back darker and thicker.

Electrolysis and laser treatments will permanently remove hair. Because it depends on the pigment in the hair to take the heat to the root, these treatments work best when there is a strong contrast between the colour of your skin and the colour of your hair. It is therefore not possible to treat tanned skin. These treatments can be painful and expensive but they are well worth it!

COSMETIC SURGERY

We would not advise cosmetic surgery. There are many types of modelling and you should find an area that suits you based on your natural looks. As you get older you may be able to move into the classic model division and if you look unnatural you will simply not be booked. Some people have Botox injections to mask ageing lines but this only works if it is subtle, so be very careful.

A very common form of surgery is breast augmentation. Although a fairly straightforward procedure, any dramatic results will affect the type of modelling you get booked for, so check with your booker before having any major cosmetic procedures. In certain types of modelling, such as glamour or lingerie, it is accepted that fake breasts are more the norm.

HYGIENE

Personal hygiene should be a high priority for any model; no one wants to work with someone who has a body odour problem. So make sure you are fresh before a shoot and carry an antiperspirant with you, and if need be take a travel wash kit, which includes a deodorant, wet wipes, and a toothbrush and paste.

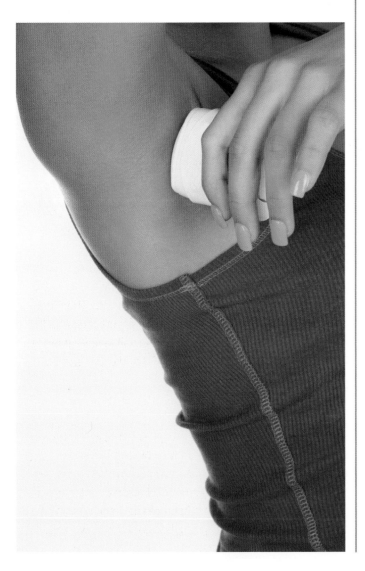

HAIR

The styles you see in magazines have taken hours to perfect so you are not expected to walk around with perfect salon-groomed hair every day. It is, however, important to ensure your hair is clean, healthy and in good condition. Have regular trims to prevent damaged split ends and use a deep conditioning treatment every three to six weeks, depending on the condition of your hair. Do not blow dry more than necessary and never rub your hair with a towel as this will damage the outer layer, causing split ends. You will find your hair is put through a lot with heated products on shoots so try to give it some time off when you are not working. It is important to find a style that suits you and works for you.

For men it is a very personal choice but just make sure your hairstyle is the same as on your photos. Getting your hair neatened every three to five weeks is advisable and clean hair is a must. Use hair products if you prefer that unwashed look!

If you wish to colour your hair get it done professionally and choose a shade that is close to your natural colour otherwise it will look very unnatural. Always consult your agent before drastically changing your colour or haircut. Remember, any major changes will mean a whole new set of pictures for your book. Never perm your hair as the chemicals are damaging and it will take a long time to grow out.

Dandruff is hormonal but can also be caused by stress or the head getting too hot. Washing your hair regularly with a good tea tree shampoo should help. Double your pillow cases and wash them and your hair towel in a hot wash to kill off the yeast which exacerbates the problem.

CLOTHES/STYLING

On a day-to-day basis you should dress according to the castings you have. This, however, can prove difficult if you have several different castings in one day.

As a model you should always look stylish and wear clothes that show off your body shape. For most castings, jeans and a tight-fitting top is usual, however, you may be asked to wear a suit or skirt so always check with your booker.

Your agency will often advise you on your image and in some cases take you shopping but it is important to feel comfortable and confident in what you wear. Also remember that as a model you tend to do a lot of walking to and from castings, so comfortable footwear is essential. Many girls wear trainers and carry heels to change into for castings.

07 finances

finances

There is no set fee for modelling work. Rates vary depending on usage and exclusivity, the type of work and the appeal of the model. It is therefore vital to have a good agent to negotiate the correct fee for each individual job. In exchange the agent will take a percentage of the model's earnings, usually around 20 per cent.

Model earnings can appear very high at first glance as the average day rate for a model is significantly higher than national averages. But you must not forget the hours you spend going to castings that are unsuccessful and the days you do not work. Although you may earn a lot one day, you may not enjoy any fee-paying work for the rest of the week, so concentrate on your yearly income rather than your day rate. Also remember your agency will take a percentage of your fee so the amount you receive will be considerably less than the amount you were quoted. The agency may also charge the client an arrangement fee, but this should not affect the model's earnings. As a model you will not normally receive any of the benefits of being a member of staff, such as holiday or sickness pay, subsidised meals or health insurance.

Rates

Advertising work pays the best as the usage is usually high. Rates are based on where and how often the image is published. For instance, an advert on a billboard poster campaign will pay a lot more than an advert in a local shop window. The rate is also dependent on the size of the advert, where it is placed, the number of times it is used and how long it runs for.

Fashion editorial modelling in national magazines pays very little. Unless you are an A-list celebrity, featuring on the cover of Vogue can earn a model as little as US$150. Models are more than willing to take this work as it gives them exposure to the higher paying advertising clients and they can also build up tear sheets for their book. These shoots tend to lead to better profile jobs.

There are many types of catalogues, from sportswear and workwear to fashion, and rates vary according to usage and circulation. Some catalogues pay several thousand dollars a day so can be very lucrative for models.

When a model agrees to be exclusive to a single company their agent is able to negotiate much higher fees for them. The model is often not allowed to work for any competitive brands for the duration of the contract so the fee must cover this loss of potential earnings. For instance, if you were to do a high profile shampoo commercial you would be known for that so other companies may not want to use you. This mostly happens with cosmetic brands as the model becomes 'the face' of the product.

Some catwalk models can command huge fees, often up to US$30,000 for a big designer show. Equally, a smaller show could pay as little as US$100. Not all catwalk shows feature big names or products; sometimes they are corporate jobs showing off in-house clothing, and these are a great way to boost your income and get some catwalk practice.

Rates also vary for more specific types of modelling. If you are unrecognisable in an image, such as shot from behind, or if the picture is blurred, you will be paid less as you are not associated with that product. This is often the case for body and parts models, and extras.

The higher your profile the more you can expect to earn. This is particularly the case for glamour modelling. The basic rates for glamour model shoots are considerably lower than commercial and advertising modelling, however, some girls manage to make a name for themselves and command very large sums. A lot of glamour work is based around personal appearances and fronting a brand. This can at times lead to celebrity status.

Some fashion models have such widespread appeal that companies fight to use them in their campaigns, leading to supermodel status. This in turn means the models can command huge sums for their work.

Promotional work can pay well and is worked out on a daily rate. Often you will be booked for a number of days at a time and sometimes even weeks. Some models earn a

respectable salary from this work alone. Usually all expenses are covered by the client, including nights in hotels and food expenses.

Most jobs will compensate you for excessive travel expenses. You will need to send your travel receipts or declare your mileage to your agency and this will be paid when you receive your job fee.

Managing your money

As a model you are self-employed. This means you are liable for paying your own tax and keeping your own accounts. At the end of each year you (or your accountant) will summarise your earnings and expenses. Deducting your expenses from your earnings gives you your profit for the year. You pay income tax and various other government taxes on your profit on a percentage basis so the more profit you make the more tax you will pay.

We strongly recommend you employ an accountant to prepare your end of year accounts. Preferably choose one who has been recommended by friends or the agency. This way they can advise you on the various legal aspects and on taxation. Many models fail to deal with this straightaway and a couple of years down the line face a large tax bill. The key point to remember is that at the end of the year you will receive a tax bill based on your earnings throughout that year. The amount you need to pay will vary depending on how much you have earned but you should try to put aside approximately 30 per cent every month.

You only pay tax on profit. If your expenses are considered to be solely related to your work, then you can deduct them from your earnings. As a self-employed person you should keep receipts for everything you spend. You would be surprised what you can claim back from your tax bill: haircuts and gym club membership to help you keep fit, clothes and make-up that you'll need for castings and modelling sessions, any work-related telephone calls, and all your marketing costs like cards and maintaining a website. Your accountant will explain all the tax exemptions. We strongly advise storing all your receipts in a safe place at the end of each day – this will save you a lot of time at the end of the tax year.

Tax forms

As you are self-employed you will have to complete a self-assessment tax form. You will hopefully have an accountant to do this for you, however, it is good to have an idea of what is involved.

'Date of commencement' means start date of your year's earnings, and 'date of cessation' is the date you finish. The easiest way is to fill in your self-assessment form online and send it by email. That way the computer will help you with the calculations and will save the details for you each year. You can, of course, fill out the form by hand, but make sure you have neat, legible handwriting. Ensure you get your tax return in on time as the authorities levy automatic fines for late filing. For more information, contact your local tax authority. No one enjoys dealing with tax and most find the forms complicated, so if you are struggling, do not worry, you are not alone!

Savings

It may be difficult to save at first as it usually takes three months for your agency to transfer your cut of a fee to your account. Most models find that at times they earn a lot of money and at others they are struggling, so plan ahead and save for a rainy day. Our advice would be to split your income three ways. For every payment you receive, a third should be allocated for monthly living expenses, such as rent or mortgage payments, residential taxes and general household bills. Another third should be spent on food and drink, and any luxuries such as clothes, cosmetics and grooming. The final third should be set aside for your tax bill. It is advisable to open a separate high-interest account for the money you are setting aside for your tax bill. A third may sound high for your tax bill but the benefit is you should have a little left after tax for savings.

Applying for a mortgage

It is perfectly feasible to apply for a mortgage if you are self-employed but it is less straightforward than if you had a job with a regular income. There are a number of ways but the easiest is to put down a large deposit – 15 per cent of the property value should guarantee a mortgage from the bank or building society, although in some cases as much as 25 per cent will be required. As someone who is self employed you will need to keep accounts, and most money lenders will ask for three years' worth of accounts. This is so they know what

you have been earning, and more importantly that you can meet your monthly repayments. You could also get a guarantor for your mortgage, someone to give the lenders security that, should you not be able to afford the repayments, they will be liable.

Try to get onto the property ladder as soon as possible. It is generally much better to be paying money back into a property than paying someone else's mortgage by renting, although renting can provide greater flexibility, especially if you are lucky enough to spend time abroad on modelling assignments. Always research the property market thoroughly though before making a purchase and make sure you can afford any payments.

terminology explained

Advance: should you ever be in need of money before your agency has been paid for a job you have done, you can ask the agency for this money as an advance. The agency will then take a percentage (usually 5%) on top of the existing percentage they take. This can seem very appealing as it is instant cash but be careful only to use this option if it is vital as you are losing money each time.

Miscellaneous expenses: you will often see this on your model statement from your agency and it includes bike fees for couriering your portfolio to prospective clients, reprints for model cards, photocopies and website update fees. Make sure you keep an eye on these as there are sometimes administrative errors and expenses you have not agreed to. Some agencies will include these expenses in their commission and some will add them as extras. Ask these questions before you join an agency.

Buy out: a buy out is a one-off fee that covers an agreement for usage of photographs in an advertisement or TV commercial you have featured in. A buy out may specify a year's usage but the client may decide to use the image the following year and therefore will pay another buy out fee. One job can sometimes be 'bought out' on several occasions.

Repeat fees: repeat fees are when you receive payment for a particular job each time it is shown on television, rather than being paid a one-off substantial fee upfront. The client will pay you each time the advert is shown. This can be financially very rewarding as the advert can often be re-used or extended from the initial agreement, and people have been known to live off one job for a year! This is a risk, however, as the commercial may get pulled earlier than expected so most agencies prefer buy outs to guarantee an agreed set fee.

08 future prospects

longevity and future prospects

As with any career, it is important to have a long-term strategy and not just focus on the weeks or months ahead. As you get older your market for modelling will naturally change. Some models will earn more and others less depending on their look and how they suit the older market.

Longevity

Edgy editorial female models for instance often find it hard to find work once they reach their mid-thirties as their look doesn't tend to suit the older commercial market. On the other hand, some commercial models in the same age bracket can earn a better living as they get older advertising family holidays, mortgage deals and luxury cars.

For a long and successful career it is important to keep your image up to date. This means improving your model portfolio, changing the way you look, and keeping up with fashion trends and looks in order to maximise your work potential. A successful model will balance high-earning jobs with high-profile jobs to work their way to bigger clients. As a model you may at times have to turn down certain jobs to avoid being typecast. For instance, if you wanted to front a campaign for a top designer you may decide to turn down catalogue work to avoid being perceived as a catalogue model by any potential future clients.

Every week new models flood the industry and competition will increase so it is essential to keep changing and improving, both with the way you present yourself and the way you look. You may even find there are times when you are not earning enough from modelling to support yourself and need to supplement your income with a non-modelling job. Try to find a job that leaves your weekdays free as most of your castings and test shoots will be done during business hours Monday to Friday. Many models get jobs as waiters or hosts in clubs and bars.

Updating your book

Your book should be constantly changing with tearsheets and test shots being added all the time. Update it regularly to keep it looking fresh and to show clients you are constantly working. The pictures you have when you first start modelling will be a lot different to those five years down the line. The way you look will change, as will the photographs you have taken of you. Your book is a selling tool and it needs to tell your clients what you are all about. If you retain old photographs in which you look a lot different from how you are now, the client will not be able to use you. Getting older and moving through the various modelling stages is not a bad thing but make sure you work closely with your booker and photographers to get it just right.

Composite cards

Your agent will produce composite cards for you to leave with potential clients at castings and, like your book, it is advisable to change these frequently. As your look or speciality evolves the photos which are best suited for your card will change. An old card suggests an out-of-work model!

Prospects and alternative careers

As with all careers, nothing in modelling is guaranteed and although you may like the idea of modelling forever it is important to think of alternative options and plan for the future. You may also find that after a few years you have achieved all you wanted to and feel it is time to move on. Modelling opens many doors to other careers in TV, film, and behind the scenes in the fashion industry as you experience many different jobs and make lots of contacts.

MODEL TURNED ACTOR (MTA)

Modelling, acting and TV work are all closely linked. Models will usually do some TV work and actors will often model products. As a model you will sometimes be given castings and auditions for TV work and feature films based on your look, but if you are serious about acting it is advisable to get a separate acting agent. Many models take acting lessons whilst modelling, and this is fully recommended as it will

help you prepare not only for any long-term acting career but also for any existing commercial castings you attend.

Acting agencies and personal managers promote their actors to casting directors and negotiate contracts on their behalf. In return they take a 10–15 per cent commission. A personal manager manages an actor's career on a more one-to-one basis. Agents represent a range of actors in age, size, height and ethnicity to ensure they fill the diverse requirements of casting directors. Never pay to join an agency and make sure you are clear about the agency's terms and commitments before signing a contract.

The acting industry is extremely competitive with thousands of actors competing for a small number of jobs, so professional training is essential for success and often for agency representation. Drama training can start at any age and should continue throughout your acting career to develop acting techniques or to prepare for a specific role.

Under 18s can attend stage schools which provide specialist training in acting, singing and dancing with full- or part-time courses. There are also drama schools for adults offering a variety of full- and part-time courses, details of which will be available in each school's prospectus or on their website. Training can be expensive and requires total commitment so make sure you really want to act for a living. Remember you can join a local dramatics society and do it for fun first!

Although there is a lot of acting in modelling it is important to remember that acting is not about being beautiful, but playing a character. As an actor you will need a head shot to promote you which will be different from the one on your model composite card as it must demonstrate the real you rather than you just looking beautiful or handsome. Keep your appearance natural so that casting directors, agents and production companies can picture you in different roles. Look straight into the camera lens and wear simple clothes and no accessories as these will detract. Do not have your hands in the shot and do not smile too much as this will make your eyes squint. Acting auditions are much more specialist than model castings and you will need to prepare more fully, learning to correctly interpret the words you use.

As an actor it is important to join a union as they protect your rights and working conditions, as well as offer advice on pay and help with legal assistance. Each country has their own actors' union. If you wish to work abroad you will need to contact the actors' union in that country to determine the employment legislation. For instance, if you wish to work in the USA you would need either a green card or to be a member of their actors' union.

PRESENTING

This is a great job if you are the type of person who enjoys being around people, however, it is not as glamorous as most people imagine. Presenting is demanding work and very competitive, and getting work and finding an agent can be a long and laborious process.

As a presenter you get to meet exciting people and go to lots of fun parties, but you are not the star and many people go into this career blinkered, thinking it will help them achieve fame. The secret to being a good presenter is being able and willing to listen and find out about other people – it's not all about you!

There are many types of presenting, from the glamorous assistant on a gameshow through to hosting a holiday show, so different types of work call for different skills. Some presenters start out as models or actors and move into presenting work, while others are experts in their field, such as designers, chefs or sports stars. Although looks are important for TV presenting, and coming from a model background can often be beneficial when getting started, it is also about the way you talk, and your personality and ability to handle the technical side of presenting, such as the auto cue and ear pieces.

Often presenters work their way up through the production side of television, starting as a runner or researcher and eventually moving into presenting. Drama schools and colleges also offer courses in presenting which is a great way to see if it is right for you. Probably the easiest way for a model to get into presenting is to make a showreel and send it to presenting agents whose job it is to promote their presenters for job opportunities and negotiate contracts on their behalf. In return they will take a 10–15 per cent commission. Never pay to join an agency and make sure you are clear about the terms of the contract before you sign anything.

Before you approach presenting agents check their client list and the area in which they specialise to ensure they are appropriate for you. Then send a CV, covering letter and recent photograph (headshot) and a showreel. Enclosing a stamped addressed envelope is also a good idea to encourage a reply!

Making a showreel

When making a showreel bear in mind that agents receive hundreds each month so make sure it is simple and indicates the type of presenting you want to do. In the early stages there is no need to pay a company to make a showreel for you. Grab a friend and a camcorder and go on to the streets. A straightforward piece to camera, an interview with a friend or family member and a simple 'walk and talk' are all that are needed to see if you've got what it takes.

- Make sure you know what kind of presenter you want to be and the type of shows you want to present, and stick to it! You can't be everything to everyone.

- Don't try to emulate the style of someone already on our screens. Nobody wants an imitation of someone already out there.

- Learn the trade. Read about the industry and make a list of production companies that make your favourite shows so that you know who to target. And practise all the time. Learn pieces to camera working to a specific time, with the radio or TV on in the background to distract you, and learn to listen whilst talking, so that when you do get that screen test, you have a better chance of getting the job.

- Go into presenting with your eyes open. We really can't stress enough that to be a success in this area takes a lot of hard work, patience and, quite often, good timing.

VOICE-OVER PRESENTERS

There are also specific agencies that specialise in promoting actors and presenters for voice-over work, mostly for commercials on TV and radio. You will need a professionally recorded voicereel with a variety of clips to demonstrate versatility and a range of accents.

PHOTOGRAPHER

As a model you will gather a lot of hands-on experience in photography as you will work with a variety of photographers and will acquire a good general knowledge of how a shoot works. Because of this many models find photography an easy transition. They also have the contacts with the clients and photographers they have gathered along the way.

If you are interested in photography modelling is a great way to get experience of shoots whilst being paid! There are many full- or part-time courses available so do your research and make sure you choose the right one for you. Digital photography has taken precedence over film photography which means set-up costs are expensive. Any equipment will need updating regularly and you will also need to take into account studio hire fees and any assistants you will need to hire.

MAKE-UP ARTIST

Some models-turned-make-up-artists can forge a very lucrative career as they already know the industry and have worked with numerous make-up artists in their modelling days so can pick up useful tricks and also learn what not to do! They also know a lot of photographers and clients so find it easy to get work. As a make-up artist you can work with the same clients and photographers over and over again, building a client base, and some models prefer this regularity and familiarity.

You will need make-up training and there are many courses on offer, from evening classes to full-time programmes to gain the qualifications needed to work as a fully qualified make-up artist. Some course fees will

include the tools and products needed to set you up whereas others will require you to purchase your own, so bear this in mind when choosing which course suits you best.

Make-up is not only limited to the world of fashion; film, TV and stage make-up are all highly specialised, so there are many options available. This is a great qualification to get in your spare time and allows you to run the two businesses in parallel as you can gain both contacts and knowledge as you move along in both careers.

BOOKER

Becoming a booker yourself is another route that a lot of models take as it is often seen as a logical progression. Invariably you will know many clients, having modelled for them through the years, you understand the terminology and have a thorough knowledge of how the industry works.

Speak with your agency, perhaps starting by working as a model scout as this is a great way to recruit models for your agency and to prove your commitment. If you do decide to make the transition from model to booker you will have to give up your job as a model.

Bookers work on commission so the money can be very good, especially once you have built up your own contacts and proved yourself.

Further education

Many models start their career at a very young age, not having completed a formal education, though some manage to fit it around their school studies. It's important to realise that a good education never goes to waste. Many models resume their education later on in life, undertaking courses in property or business, advertising or drama. Some models speak many languages and are academically highly qualified. Think carefully as to which course of study you decide to embark on as it will require hard work and a lot of commitment.

Investing in property

Bricks and mortar can make a sound long-term investment as property tends to go up in value. There may be slumps in the economy but in the long run property is often a much better option than a high-interest bank account and can provide an excellent way to supplement your income. A property will provide you with a stable base, but do not overstretch yourself financially.

If you buy a two-bedroom property you could rent out one of the bedrooms. There are always models needing accommodation so having a second bedroom should not be a worry. Buying a property is likely to be one of the biggest investments of your life, so make sure you know and understand the market and the area you are buying into. If you are astute you could even start a mini empire of your own, buying, doing up, renting and selling property at a profit.

Another way to supplement your income is to rent out your property for photo shoots and TV shows – this is not for everyone as you will have strangers in your house moving furniture around – but if you have an empty house during the day, then it's a fantastic way to generate extra income. Large, versatile open spaces are always sought after. Keep the space clean, simple and minimalist. Quite often the money can be equal, if not more, than a model's day rate!

glossary

Advance: the modelling agency pays the model fee (or part of the fee) in advance of receiving money from the client. This often incurs a 5 per cent commission.

Agency: the office from which model bookers work.

Agent: person who manages a model's career.

Art director: directs photo shoots and is the first point of contact for the client.

Assistant: person assigned to assist the photographer on photo shoots.

Audition: similar to a casting but often involves learning a script or reading for a part for a TV assignment.

Book: another word for a portfolio.

Booker: point of contact at the agency. A booker will book shoots, organise diaries and look after the general welfare of models.

Booking: confirmed job given to a model by the agent.

Book out: booking a day off work in advance.

Buy-out: one-off payment allowing specific usage of an image or commercial.

Call sheet: all the information needed in writing for a shoot day and given to a model.

Campaign: when a model becomes the face of a product.

Card or composite card: selection of pictures taken from a portfolio and featured on one card.

Casting: meeting with potential clients.

Casting director: person who allocates a specific job to a model.

Catalogue work: model appears in catalogues, modelling clothing for instance.

Cattle call: when a number of models turn up for the same job casting whether they are suitable or not.

Chart: model's diary kept by the agency.

Check in: phoning the agency at the end of the day to check castings for the following day.

Clean face: for women, no make-up; for men, clean shaven.

Client: person directly responsible for a shoot.

Commercial: television advert.

Contract: binding agreement between a model and an agency/client.

Day rate: fee a model commands for a day's work.

Edgy: describes a model with strong, unusual features.

Editorial: print work in magazines.

Fashion week: week in which designers unveil their new collections.

Fee: money paid for a job.

Fitting: getting clothing sized for a particular job.

Full length: photographic shot that shows the whole body, head to toe.

General: casting for models when they have not been specifically requested.

Go see: when a model meets potential clients should any work arise in the future. It's more of a meet and greet than a specific job opportunity.

Head booker: main booker in charge of either the male or female team of bookers.

Head shot: head and shoulders only shot.

High fashion: haute couture. Premium clothing range.

List: sheet models write their names on when they walk into a casting to determine the casting order so no one jumps the queue.

Make-up artist: person in charge of grooming a model for a photo shoot.

Model release: form signed by a model giving rights to a client or photographer to publish their pictures.

In-house: internal modelling for a company, usually consisting of fittings.

On location: shooting away from a studio.

Open call: a casting at which models are not specifically requested so anyone can attend.

Option: job not yet confirmed but with a high level of interest from a client.

Parts model: modelling that focuses on specific body parts, such as feet or hands.

Pencilled: vague interest shown by a client in booking a model for a job.

Polaroid: quick unprofessional snapshot for the client's reference.

Re-call: when a model is asked to go back to see a client.

Repeat fees: fee a model receives every time their image is used.

Request: when a model has been requested by a client to attend a casting.

Showreel: short film showcasing clips from any film, TV or commercial work completed.

Stylist: person in charge of clothing the model on a shoot.

Tearsheet: pages from published work.

Ten by eight: size of print (in inches).

Testing: getting new photographs done to add to a portfolio.

Usage: where and how often pictures are shown, as agreed by the client and agent.

Visa: legal document allowing you to work in a foreign country.

Zed card: card with a selection of pictures from a portfolio. It is the same as a composite card.

model agencies

EUROPE

www.bossmodels.cz (Czech Republic)
www.scoop-models.com (Denmark)
www.balticmodels.com (Estonia)
www.contrebande.com (France)
www.louisa-models.de (Germany)
www.modelwerk.com (Germany)
www.pmamodels.com (Germany)
www.acemodels.gr (Greece)
www.i-m.gr (Greece)
www.assetmodels.com (Ireland)
www.fashion-elite.com (Italy)
www.fashionmodel.it (Italy)
www.whynotmodels.com (Italy)
www.euromodel.nl (Netherlands)
www.touchemodels.com (Netherlands)
www.ullamodels.com (Netherlands)
www.gomodelsagency.com (Portugal)
www.marlylinagency.com (Spain)
www.upmodels.com (Sweden)
www.models1.co.uk (UK)
www.modelteam.co.uk (UK)
www.stormmodels.com (UK)

NORTH AND SOUTH AMERICA

www.fordmodels.com.br (Brazil)
www.lequipeagence.com.br (Brazil)
www.majoragency.com (Brazil)
www.elitemodel.com (Canada)
www.iconmodels.ca (Canada)
www.nextmodels.ca (Canada)
www.stylusmodels.com (Canada)
www.bossmodels.com (USA)
www.fordmodels.com (USA)
www.lamodels.com (USA)
www.lookmodelagency.com (USA)
www.nextmodelsusa.com (USA)
www.trumpmodels.com (USA)
www.wilhemina.com (USA)

AUSTRALASIA

www.bodyworxmodels.com.au (Australia)
www.chadwickmodels.com (Australia)
www.scenemodels.com (Australia)
www.62models.com (New Zealand)
www.nova-models.co.nz (New Zealand)

ASIA

www.modelsHK.com (Hong Kong)
www.elitemodelsindia.com (India)
www.image-models.com (Israel)
www.cdumodels.com (Japan)
www.modusvivendis.ru (Russia)
www.elite-singapore.com (Singapore)
www.mannequin.com.sg (Singapore)
www.bareface.net (UAE)
http://connectedmodels.com (UAE)

AFRICA

www.maxmodels.co.za (Cape Town, South Africa)

the authors

Louise Cole can be seen on GMTV most mornings modelling the latest fashions. She has appeared in fashion shows and in press and poster advertisements for Burberry, Harvey Nichols, Gossard Wonderbra, Nicole Farhi, One-2-One, Harley Davidson, Argos, Boots, Littlewoods, BT, Gap, Muller Light, Tesco, Snow and Rock, Aquafresh, Aquafresh, Volvo, Stella McCartney, Asda, Golf, Wella, Marks & Spencer, Currys, and Miele. She has graced the covers of numerous magazines, books and CDs as well as appearing in TV commercials for sport, cars, fashion and lingerie, and in several music videos. She was also a Miss Great Britain finalist in 2006.

Louise competed in the National Trampolining championships and specialises in sports modelling. She has featured in numerous campaigns including Nike, Puma and Adidas.

Louise's TV presenting work includes The Ultimate Playboy, with model Jodie Kidd. She was the trampolinist in the Bond film Tomorrow Never Dies, and also featured as Miss France in the film Action Star.

Louise is not just a pretty face as she graduated with a BSc Honours Degree in Psychology from Loughborough University.

PICTURE CREDITS:

Amarang (p 7), Corbis (pp 9, 10, 11, 80, 81).

Giles Vickers-Jones has fronted campaigns for Suits You, Remington, Rubicon, Pencarnie, Toni & Guy, L'Oreal and Littlewoods. He has also done a great deal of magazine work, including appearances in Fluid, Glamour, Company and FHM.

Having made the transition from modelling to presenting, Giles has completed various TV shows for British and US television, including the long running ITV at the Movies, having completed over 75 episodes in three years. He has also presented numerous dating, music and morning shows in the UK as well as a weekly showbiz show for E! in the US. As well as his TV career, Giles has other writing credits to his name, including two other books and a high profile film column. As an active campaigner for the environment, he has an eco-business called pixeltrees.com with the aim of saving a million trees in the rain forest.

CREDITS:

Special thanks to Corinne for her patience and support. Humfrey, our book agent, Paul Stacey Management, Rita Westenius, Hugh Harris, Andy Lesauvage for his photography magic, Gilad Wolfin, Simon Powell, Pete Webb, MOT Models, Eric Caffyn, Kirsty Spence, Melissa Bullock, Sasha Abraham, Glo beauty salon in Fulham and the modelling industry for all our exciting experiences. Remembering Azabold, Rodney, Michael Vickers-Jones and Annie Loudon.

Finally, to all our friends and family: a big thank you for your continuous love and support.

index